INSTANT COOKING

JILL McWILLIAM

OCTOPUS BOOKS
IN ASSOCIATION WITH BEJAM

Right Seafood pasta (page 24)
Front cover: Sesame chicken kebabs;
(page 25); Ham and peanut salad (page 46)
Back cover: Sausage and baked bean pasties (page 46)

ACKNOWLEDGMENTS

Recipes developed by: Sue Ross

Editors: Eve Dowling, Diana Craig

Copy editor: Jenni Fleetwood

Art editor: David Rowley

Designer: Michelle Stamp

Photographer: Chris Crofton

Stylist: Marian Price

Food prepared for photography by: Lorna Rhodes

For their kindness in providing materials used in the photography

for this book, the publishers would like to thank:

Villeroy and Boch, Regent Street, London W1

NOTES

Standard spoon measurements are used in all recipes:
1 tablespoon = one 15 ml spoon
1 teaspoon = one 5 ml spoon
All spoon measures are level.
All eggs are size 3 (standard) unless otherwise stated.
For all recipes, quantities are given in both metric and imperial measures.
Follow either set but not a mixture of both, as they are not interchangeable.

All recipes include preparation and cooking time (excluding thawing time).
The instructions also indicate whether all or part of each recipe can be made
in the microwave cooker, and whether or not the recipes can be frozen.
Microwave instructions are for a 600W microwave cooker.

Published by Octopus Books Limited,
59 Grosvenor Street, London W1X 9DA

First published 1987
© Octopus Books 1987
ISBN 0 7064 2863 3

Printed in Hong Kong

CONTENTS

MAKING THE MOST OF TIME

Time is the one ingredient all too often in short supply in today's world of working women, one-parent households and families with diverse interests. Sitting down together for a meal with all the family is a rare treat nowadays. Dad may be off to his French class, Mum to her course in car maintenance (or the other way round), and children may have sporting fixtures or social engagements to go to. With such hectic lifestyles, you will want to make the most of the time you do have together, so we have produced this book to help you do just that.

Instant food need not be boring or predictable, as a look through these pages will show you – yet all the dishes here can be made in 30 minutes or less, so in half an hour you could have a meal on the table that will make sure your family stays home more often! Impromptu entertaining will be easier, too. When friends drop in on the spur of the moment, imagine their amazement when you offer to 'knock up a little something' in the kitchen, only to emerge a short while later with an impressive spread fit for a king.

Of course, none of this can be achieved by magic and, as any magician will tell you, behind the illusion lies planning, organization and having the proper equipment. To make sure that you can always come up with the right ingredient at the right time, it's essential to have a well-stocked freezer and store cupboard . . . and organized shopping is the way to keep them that way. Having a running list of things that will soon need replacing is a good habit to get into, so that you don't have to waste time popping out for individual items.

With a microwave cooker as well as a freezer, you have the perfect combination for instant success in the kitchen. Frozen items can be whipped out of the freezer to be thawed at a moment's notice, and then either cooked in the conventional way or, for even greater speed, in the microwave. If you have no microwave, a little advance planning will ensure that ingredients are thawed in time for cooking.

With this book on your kitchen shelf, and your freezer and perhaps microwave cooker to help you, feeding family and friends will be easier, quicker, and a lot more enjoyable for the cook, too!

Jun McWilliam

Although few of us have time for leisurely cooking, our busy lives do not mean that we cannot eat well. For a continuous source of good food, few kitchen aids can be more helpful than the freezer – but to make it work for you, you must keep it properly stocked.

STOCKING THE FREEZER

Here is an alphabetical list of some of the most useful items for your freezer. Consult it next time you compile your shopping list.

Bread

Sliced loaves can be toasted straight from the freezer and both whole loaves and rolls can be successfully thawed in the microwave cooker, if you have one, or at room temperature. Frozen french-style baguettes can be sliced and used to make a quick crusty topping for soups and stews. And frozen garlic bread makes a super standby for unexpected suppers.

Breadcrumbs

Store these in a sealed polythene bag and use as little or as much as you need in puddings, stuffings and bread sauces. To use as a topping or coating, thaw and dry them in the microwave cooker.

Cheese

Don't throw away scraps of cheese: keep any leftover pieces for the freezer. A mixture of different cheeses can make a tasty sauce.

Cream

To freeze successfully, cream must contain 40 per cent butterfat, so choose double or whipping cream, plus a carton or two of whipped cream. Alternatively buy ready-frozen cream which is conveniently frozen into short pieces for easy measuring and quick thawing. Use frozen cream to add a touch of luxury to tinned or packet soups.

Eggs

Whole eggs aren't worth freezing (and must never be frozen in the shell) but egg whites freeze well and are useful for meringues and toppings. Freeze egg whites without beating, in sealed rigid containers, for up to 6 months. Thaw quickly and easily in the microwave cooker, or at room temperature.

Fish

The choice of fish is up to you but it is a good idea to keep a packet or two of prime cod or haddock fillets in addition to your personal favourites. Fish thaws quickly in the microwave cooker and many varieties can be cooked from frozen (check packet instructions). It cooks swiftly too, so is one of the most useful standbys for the hostess in a hurry. Prawns are also invaluable, and when you have a packet in the freezer you can defrost the exact quantity you require, whether it be 500g (1¼lb) for prawns in garlic butter (page 14) or just a couple to garnish a starter or snack.

Fresh herbs

Herbs take up very little room in your freezer and are well worth storing. Freeze your own and use whole or crumble while frozen (which saves chopping).

Fruit

Purée frozen fruit to make sauces, or blend with milk and a little honey or sugar to make delicious, fresh-tasting milkshakes. Do not forget frozen Jaffa orange juice either – it comes in handy for sorbets.

Ice creams

There can be few freezers that don't boast at least one tub of ice cream. Another gift to the cook-cum-conjuror, vanilla ice cream can be turned into dozens of dreamy desserts with the addition of puréed fruit, liqueurs or sauces (see some of the ideas on pages 38-41). Keep some of the luxury ice creams such as Chocolate and orange with Cointreau, and Irish coffee with whiskey, for sundaes and high days and holidays.

Ice cubes

Make plenty in advance for summer drinks or parties. Add a shot of soda water to keep them apart when storing.

Lemon juice

When lemons are cheap, squeeze some and store the juice in ice cube trays. Lemon slices freeze well, too, as do orange slices. Open freeze, then store in sealed polythene bags. Citrus fruit segments or slices may be frozen for up to 10 months.

Meat
Buy just what you and your family enjoy and keep a look out for boneless diced meats – a great time-saver. Don't forget the hamburgers and steakgrills – they are quick to cook for all the family and you can always ring the changes by giving them different toppings (see pages 21 and 28).

Pastry
All types of pastry are worth freezing and it's a good idea to keep a couple of flan cases for quick fills.

Pizzas
Children love them and for adult guests you can add sophisticated toppings such as clams and mushrooms or artichoke hearts and Parma ham.

Poultry
Small cuts make sense when speed is of the essence, and boneless portions take up less space than whole birds.

Ready meals
Make double the quantity of whatever you are cooking, freeze half, and you will always have something on hand for times when you don't feel like cooking.

Sauces
Sweet and savoury sauces store well and help to make a quick pie filling, topping or accompaniment.

Sausages
Sausages can be cooked from frozen. Make them a little different by wrapping each in a slice of bacon first.

Savoury butters
Use on steak, chops or fish (or try with vegetables) for that professional touch.

Stock
Keep a small quantity of concentrated stock in the freezer for soups and sauces. Fish stock is particularly worthwhile since it is not readily available in cans or cubes.

Vegetables
Keep up to date with additions to the range

of frozen vegetables; there are many speciality vegetable mixes now available, such as Oriental Mix which combines a selection of exotic vegetables – ideal for a speedy stir fry. And don't miss the Stewpacks, a mixture of prime root vegetables that will save you a lot of scrubbing and peeling next time you want to make a stew or casserole.

Vegetarian meals
Keep some of these on hand for unexpected guests or unsuspected vegetarians! You and your family will enjoy them too.

STOCKING THE STORE CUPBOARD
Having the right staples in the store cupboard makes spur-of-the-moment cooking easy. Pantry preferences are highly personal, but here are some suggestions.

There are some essentials that it is easy to forget about, but which it is extremely annoying to run out of at a crucial moment – baking powder, cream of tartar, bicarbonate of soda and dried yeast, for example.

A supply of sauces, such as soy, tomato ketchup and Worcestershire, is always handy for giving dishes a quick pick-up in flavour, and mustard is especially good for intensifying the taste of cheese sauce.

Coffee can be used in the same way to bring out the taste of chocolate, and it is worth keeping a stock of cooking chocolate, too. Grated, it makes a quick topping for cold desserts or cakes, and melted chocolate makes a delicious instant sauce for ice cream or fruit.

A selection of biscuits, like sponge fingers, ratafias and langues de chat, are useful for making spontaneous sweets or as accompaniments, and digestive biscuits make a quick crust for sweet pies or cheesecakes.

Other obvious items to keep in the store cupboard are herbs, jams, honey, tinned fruits (for puddings and pie fillings), tinned soups (for instant sauces), flours, oils, mayonnaise, rice and pasta.

KITCHEN HELPERS
Which are the appliances that really help to save time?

Microwave cookers
Top of the list must be the microwave cooker. Although exciting in its own right, it really comes into its own as an adjunct to other kitchen appliances and you will probably bless it most heartily when it softens butter, warms rolls, reheats your coffee, dries croûtons, melts chocolate, rehydrates dried fruits, or even warms the baby's bottle – the list is endless and as you grow to love your microwave cooker you will add your own plus points.

The value of a microwave cooker as a means of rapidly thawing frozen food has already been mentioned (see 'Stocking the freezer'), and it can also make individual diets easy to cater for. Different members of the same family may have diverse dietary requirements. One may be trying to slim, another adopting a special eating regime while training for sport, a third avoiding eggs or dairy products. You may have a diabetic child who needs frequent small meals or an elderly relative who cannot cope with highly spiced food.

The convenience, versatility and cleanliness of microwave cookers is perfectly demonstrated on pages 54-69. Many of the other recipes in this book also include a 'Microspot' – tips to help you make better use of your microwave cooker.

Blenders
These have practically become standard kitchen equipment and need no introduction. They are invaluable time savers, their main disadvantage being the

job of cleaning after use. Do consider the hand-held blenders now on the market. They are highly efficient, can blend very small amounts in any container from cup to saucepan and are easily rinsed under the tap to get them clean.

Mixers and food processors

There are devotees of large food mixers and there are fans of food processors, although the two appliances are not interchangeable. Unless you can afford both, plump for an efficient hand-held food mixer with sturdy beaters, and a well-designed food processor. And remember, it's no use keeping your food processor in a cupboard – it needs to be close at hand for immediate use. Have it on the work surface, preferably permanently plugged in. Get into the habit of using it regularly and it may be one of your best allies in the race against time.

A HEALTHY RESPECT

Fast food needn't be unhealthy food. Frozen food, for example, retains a very high percentage of its nutrients, natural colour and flavour. With the wide range of frozen foods now available all year round, your diet need never be boring – you can eat the healthy, appetizing food of your choice whatever the season.

Couple your freezer with a microwave cooker and you have a partnership which will delight your family for many years to come. The microwave cooker can be the means of introducing your family to a healthier diet. Foods are cooked with little or no fats, salt is kept to a minimum as foods retain far more of their natural flavours, and few nutrients are lost, thanks to short cooking times with little or no added water.

Bejam have a serious commitment to encourage their customers to eat a healthy, balanced diet and are constantly looking at ways of improving their products in this respect. They set up their Healthy Eating Advisory Service with the help of independent nutritionist Dr Juliet Gray for precisely this reason. Their booklet 'Food Facts' is packed with nutritional information on their products. On looking through the booklet, customers can see at a glance that few Bejam products contain artificial colouring or additives.

TRICKS AND TREATS

When it comes to high-speed entertaining there are plenty of perfectly honest little tricks that can gently persuade your guests you have spent hours preparing for their visit. With this book at your fingertips you will have plenty of ideas for spectacularly simple and quick meals but here are a few extra ideas for instant success:

Keep a packet of frozen smoked salmon in the freezer. Serve simply on slices of brown bread and butter or stir into scrambled egg for a special starter.

Frozen pastry is a gift to the busy cook. Try frozen vol-au-vents with a quick, fishy filling. Cook a packet of cod in mushroom sauce according to the instructions on the packet. Flake the cod in the sauce and stir in a little white wine and a few thawed frozen prawns.

Or impress your guests with croûtes made using 225 g (8 oz) frozen puff pastry. Thaw the pastry, roll it out and cut into 4 squares, each measuring 6×6 cm (2½×2½ inches). With a sharp knife, score a square within each square. Bake the pastry squares on a baking sheet in a preheated hot oven (220°C, 425°F, Gas Mark 7) for 25 minutes or until the pastry is golden. Remove the shells from the baking sheet and cut out and discard the centres. Fill with one of the following:

★ frozen Ratatouille (or the equivalent weight of stewed tomatoes, aubergines, courgettes, sweet red and green peppers and onions) cooked and topped with grated cheese
★ 175 g (6 oz) frozen cod in mushroom sauce, cooked according to packet instructions and with the fish flaked.
★ frozen prawns, thawed and combined with 300 ml (½ pint) white sauce and a pinch of tarragon
★ 250 g (9 oz) frozen Sweet 'n' Sour Chicken cooked according to packet instructions.

Frozen vegetables can be a clever cook's closest companions, and can be used in imaginative combinations for fresh appeal. For a gourmet touch, try:

★ frozen green beans with toasted almonds
★ frozen mange tout peas with sautéed

sweet red pepper rings
★ frozen broccoli with mushrooms and celery
★ frozen cauliflower with crisply fried wholewheat breadcrumbs
★ frozen spinach with diced spring onions
★ frozen baby onions, glazed in butter with a little sugar

Pitta bread is perfect for parties and other occasions when a snack in the hand is worth two on the plate. Serve pittas filled with mini meatballs, salad, sliced salmon or smoked trout – the choice is yours.

Crêpes – both savoury and sweet – are a useful freezer standby. Try them filled with Chili bean mix, cooked according to packet instructions, for a vegetarian meal that's as simple to make as it is satisfying. For a quick pudding, fill sweet crêpes with cooked and sweetened frozen apples, blackcurrants or cherries and serve with ice cream or frozen and thawed whipped cream.

Ice cream can be transformed into dozens of delicious desserts, including bombes, alaskas and sundaes. Try simply adding a dash of liqueur for a special occasion or top with a livener like sultanas soaked in rum. Alternatively serve with a deceptively easy sauce made by melting 100 g (4 oz) plain chocolate with 4 tablespoons golden syrup and 1 tablespoon thawed frozen cream.

For another quick dinner party dessert using ice cream, drench a sliced Arctic Roll in sherry or liqueur (Benedictine is a good choice), place in a foil-lined grill pan and top with partially thawed frozen raspberries. Cover completely with sweetened stiffly beaten egg white then cook under a preheated medium grill until the meringue peaks are golden. Remove with a fish slice and serve immediately.

Frozen fruit means desserts are always on ice. Thaw 450 g (1 lb) dark cherries and combine with the same quantity of peeled fresh lychees for a wonderful sweet that looks sensational and tastes divine.

FAMILY FARE
As well as being a boon when entertaining, a good basic stock of frozen foods will help you produce appetizing and wholesome family meals in minutes.

Top frozen fillets of haddock with a mixture of grated cheese and breadcrumbs. Dot with butter and bake in a preheated moderate oven (180°C, 350°F, Gas Mark 4) for 20-25 minutes.

If you have rice and smoked haddock in your freezer you can brighten a Sunday evening with a quick kedgeree. Cook 500 g (1¼ lb) easy-cook frozen rice according to packet instructions. Poach 225 g (8 oz) frozen smoked haddock in milk. Flake the haddock into a bowl, stir in the rice and add 1 chopped onion cooked in butter and 2 chopped hard-boiled eggs. Fold through 3 tablespoons single cream and serve hot.

It makes sense to have frozen sausages on hand for quick meals. They make terrific kebabs, particularly popular with children. Slice them thickly, thread on skewers, alternately with par-cooked mini corn on the cobs and baby tomatoes, and grill until the sausages are cooked, basting the corn and tomatoes with melted butter from time to time.

Vegetarian meals are well worth stocking and can easily be dressed up for non-vegetarian suppers. Enjoy Cauliflower cheese topped with grilled bacon, or Vegetable lasagne with rolled ham cornets.

Sliced bread can be used straight from the freezer and has umpteen applications. Dip it in a mixture of egg and milk and fry in hot butter for a tasty, hasty breakfast treat with bacon. Substitute cream for the milk and add a sprinkling of brown sugar and it becomes a sweet dish reminiscent of nursery teas. A frozen baguette or garlic bread, thickly sliced, makes a quick topping for a casserole – and if you spread the bread with French mustard and add a generous dusting of grated cheese you can upgrade the simplest stew to celebrity status.

For a tasty teatime treat roll out frozen and thawed puff pastry to a neat rectangle about 5 mm (¼ inch) thick. Sprinkle with dried fruit (raisins, sultanas, currants) and top with 3 tablespoons sugar mixed with 2 teaspoons mixed spice. Roll up, Swiss roll fashion, and chill for 30 minutes. Cut in 5 mm (¼ inch) slices and place on a baking sheet. Glaze with egg white and sugar and bake for 10-15 minutes in a preheated very hot oven (230°C, 450°F, Gas Mark 8).

STARTERS & SNACKS

Whether it's an instant snack you're after to quell the pangs of hunger at the end of your busy day, or something quick to begin a more substantial meal, here are some ideas to whet your appetite – from unusual starters to hearty soups that need only crusty bread and perhaps some cheese to provide a family meal-in-a-minute.

CREAM OF ASPARAGUS SOUP

SERVES 4
PREPARATION & COOKING TIME: 20 Minutes

50 g (2 oz) butter

100 g (4 oz) frozen onion slices, or
1 small fresh onion, peeled
and sliced

1 kg (2 lb) frozen asparagus spears, partially
thawed and chopped

1 tablespoon plain flour

350 ml (12 fl oz) boiling water

1 chicken stock cube

salt

freshly ground black pepper

600 ml (1 pint) milk

150 ml (¼ pint) single cream

1. Melt the butter in a saucepan. Add the onion slices and cook over medium heat until the onion is soft.

2. Stir in the asparagus, then sprinkle over the flour and cook the mixture for 30 seconds without allowing the mixture to brown.

3. In a jug, mix the boiling water with the stock cube. Gradually add this stock to the asparagus mixture, stirring constantly over low heat until smooth. Bring the soup to the boil and season to taste. Reduce the heat and simmer for 5-10 minutes until the asparagus is tender.

4. Purée the soup in a blender or food processor, or press through a sieve.

5. Return to the clean saucepan, add the milk and reheat without boiling.

6. Stir in the cream and return to the heat for 1-2 minutes. Serve immediately or cool and chill until required.

Note: *do not allow the soup to boil after the cream has been added as this may spoil the flavour.*

Microspot: *steps 5 and 6 may be completed in the microwave cooker. Pour the puréed mixture into a casserole or china soup tureen, add the milk and microwave, covered, for 2 minutes on HIGH, stirring after 1 minute. Stir in the cream and serve at once or leave to chill if the soup is to be served cold.*

To freeze: *omit the cream, cool the soup quickly and pour into a rigid container, leaving 2 cm (¾ inch) headspace. Seal and freeze for up to 3 months. To thaw and re-heat in the microwave cooker, place the block in a large bowl. Cover with greaseproof paper and heat on HIGH for 15-20 minutes, breaking up the block of soup as it thaws. Stir in the cream and serve.*

MINTED PEA SOUP

SERVES 4

PREPARATION & COOKING TIME: 20 Minutes

50 g (2 oz) butter

100 g (4 oz) frozen onion slices, or 1 small fresh onion, peeled and sliced

1 clove garlic, crushed

500 g (1 ¼ lb) frozen petits pois or garden peas

1.2 litres (2 pints) boiling water

1 chicken stock cube

salt

freshly ground black pepper

150 ml (¼ pint) milk

150 ml (¼ pint) single cream

1 tablespoon chopped fresh mint

1. Melt the butter in a saucepan and lightly fry the onion and garlic until soft. Remove from the heat and add the peas.

2. In a jug, mix the boiling water and the stock cube. Add to the pan, return to the heat and bring the mixture to the boil. Reduce the heat and simmer for about 4 minutes until the peas are just tender.

3. Purée in a blender or food processor or press through a sieve. Return to the clean saucepan, season to taste and stir in the milk. Reheat until just simmering.

4. Stir in the cream and serve hot, sprinkled with the fresh mint.

Note: *do not allow the soup to boil after the cream has been added.*

Microspot: *the soup may be completed in the microwave cooker. Follow the instructions under Cream of asparagus soup (page 10).*

To freeze: *follow the instructions under Cream of asparagus soup (page 10).*

Above left Minted pea soup; *Right* Seafood chowder (page 12)

DIJON MUSHROOM SOUP

SERVES 4
PREPARATION & COOKING TIME: 15 Minutes

50 g (2 oz) butter

100 g (4 oz) frozen onion slices, or 1 small fresh
onion, peeled and sliced

1 clove garlic, crushed

450 g (1 lb) frozen sliced mushrooms

500 ml (18 fl oz) boiling water

1 chicken stock cube

salt

freshly ground black pepper

1 tablespoon Dijon mustard

600 ml (1 pint) milk

150 ml (¼ pint) single cream

1. Melt the butter in a saucepan and lightly fry the onion and garlic until soft.

2. Stir in the mushrooms and cook gently for 1 minute.

3. In a jug, mix the boiling water and the stock cube. Add to the saucepan and bring the mixture to the boil over medium heat. Season to taste and stir in the mustard. Reduce the heat and simmer the soup for 2 minutes.

4. Purée the soup in a blender or food processor or press through a sieve.

5. Return the soup to the clean saucepan, stir in the milk and reheat gently until just below boiling point. Remove from the heat and stir in the cream.

6. Serve immediately, with crusty French bread if liked.

Microspot: *to warm French bread in the microwave cooker, thickly slice a half baguette and arrange the chunks of bread in a circle around the rim of a cardboard plate. Cover loosely with a napkin and microwave on LOW for 1¼-2 minutes.*

To freeze: *follow the instructions under Cream of asparagus soup (page 10).*

SEAFOOD CHOWDER

SERVES 4
PREPARATION & COOKING TIME: 17 Minutes

2 thick slices white bread

2 tablespoons vegetable oil

300 g (11 oz) can condensed chicken soup

1 tablespoon tomato purée

300 ml (½ pint) milk

200 ml (7 fl oz) water

1 tomato, skinned, seeded and chopped

salt

freshly ground black pepper

100 g (4 oz) frozen prawns

100 g (4 oz) frozen queen scallops

100 g (4 oz) frozen Ocean Stix, thawed and flaked

2 tablespoons dry sherry

150 ml (¼ pint) single cream

1. Cut the bread into 2.5 cm (1 inch) rounds. Heat the oil in a frying pan and fry the bread until golden and crisp. Drain on paper towels and set aside.

2. Mix the chicken soup, tomato purée, milk, water and tomato in a saucepan. Place over gentle heat and stir until well combined.

3. Bring to the boil, reduce the heat, season to taste and add the shellfish and sherry. Simmer very gently for 1-2 minutes.

4. Add the cream, reheat gently and serve, garnished with the croûtons.

Note: *do not allow the soup to boil after the shellfish and cream have been added.*

Microspot: *the microwave cooker makes skinning a tomato simple. Place the tomato on a paper towel and microwave on HIGH for 10-15 seconds. Allow to STAND for 5 minutes. The tomato skin can then easily be removed.*

To freeze: *see Cream of asparagus soup (page 10).*

MEXICAN BEAN SOUP

SERVES 4
PREPARATION & COOKING TIME: 27 Minutes

4 tablespoons oil

25 g (1 oz) butter

100 g (4 oz) frozen onion slices, or 1 small fresh onion, sliced

1 clove garlic, crushed

½ teaspoon chili powder

450 g (1 lb) frozen Mexican Mix, or the equivalent weight of fresh prepared diced sweet red and green peppers, corn and diced onion

1 litre (1¾ pints) boiling water

2 beef stock cubes

397 g (14 oz) can tomatoes, chopped, juice reserved

432 g (15¾ oz) can red kidney beans, drained

salt

freshly ground black pepper

grated Parmesan cheese

1. Heat the oil and butter together in a heavy-based saucepan. Add the onion and garlic and fry gently for 1-2 minutes.

2. Stir in the chili powder and cook for 30 seconds. Add all the remaining ingredients except the seasoning and cheese.

3. Bring the soup slowly to the boil, adjust the seasoning, reduce the heat and simmer for 10-15 minutes.

4. Serve each portion sprinkled with grated cheese.

Note: *for a less chunky soup, purée half the mixture in a blender or food processor and return to the saucepan with the rest of the soup. Reheat and serve.*

Microspot: *serve with tortillas, if liked. Wrap 4 tortillas in a napkin and microwave on HIGH for 1-2 minutes. If you keep them covered, they will stay soft and warm.*

To freeze: *follow the instructions under Cream of asparagus soup (page 10).*

CRISPY COD GRATIN

SERVES 2
PREPARATION & COOKING TIME: 25 Minutes

3× 170 g (6 oz) packets frozen cod in cheese sauce

1 tablespoon lemon juice

1 tablespoon dry sherry

salt

freshly ground black pepper

5 tablespoons fresh white breadcrumbs

4 tablespoons grated Cheddar cheese

lemon slices, to garnish

1. Cook the cod according to the packet instructions. Open the packets and turn the fish into a bowl. Lightly flake the cod.

2. Stir in the lemon juice and sherry and season if liked.

3. Spoon the mixtue into 2 individual ovenproof dishes or 4 scallop shells.

4. Mix the breadcrumbs and grated cheese together and sprinkle over each dish. Place under a preheated hot grill until the topping is crisp and golden. Garnish with lemon slices and serve immediately.

Variation: *as a substitute for some of the cod, use an equivalent weight of any mixture of shellfish from prawns to crab, lobster or mussels.*

Microspot: *the cod may be cooked in the microwave cooker. Pierce the boil-in bag, place it on a plate and microwave on HIGH for 5½ minutes, flexing the bag once during the process.*

To freeze: *not suitable for freezing.*

BAKED PLAICE FINGERS IN GARLIC BUTTER

SERVES 4

PREPARATION & COOKING TIME: 11 Minutes

75 g (3 oz) unsalted butter

450 g (1 lb) frozen plaice fillets, thawed and cut into 7.5 cm (3 inch) strips

3 fat cloves garlic, crushed

3 tablespoons lemon juice

3 tablespoons chopped fresh parsley

salt

freshly ground black pepper

1. Melt the butter in a large, shallow heat-proof dish. Add the plaice strips and turn to coat them evenly with butter.

2. Spread the fish out to a single layer and sprinkle them with crushed garlic and lemon juice.

3. Cook under a preheated hot grill for 1-2 minutes until the fish is hot but not dried out.

4. Sprinkle with parsley, season to taste and serve on small hot plates. Spoon the garlic butter juices over the top of each portion.

Note: *white crusty rolls make a good accompaniment. Alternatively serve on a bed of cooked rice.*

Microspot: *to thaw the fish in the microwave cooker, place on a plate, cover and micro-wave on DEFROST for 5 minutes, separating and rearranging once during the process.*

To freeze: *pour the plaice fingers and garlic butter into a rigid container, cover and freeze for up to 1 month. Reheat gently from frozen in a heavy-based saucepan for 20-25 minutes.*

Right Smoked fish and cucumber pâté

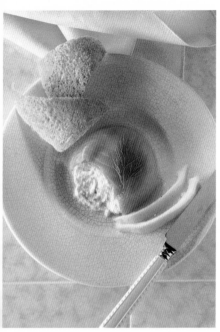

SMOKED FISH AND CUCUMBER PÂTÉ

SERVES 4
PREPARATION & COOKING TIME: 30 Minutes

225 g (8 oz) frozen smoked trout, thawed
100 g (4 oz) low fat soft cheese
100 g (4 oz) cucumber, chopped
1 tablespoon lemon juice
salt
freshly ground black pepper
175g (6 oz) frozen smoked salmon slices, thawed
TO GARNISH:
lemon slices
sprigs of dill
melba toast, to serve

1. Flake the smoked trout into a large bowl, removing any skin or bones.

2. Beat in the cheese, cucumber, lemon juice and seasoning to taste. Continue to beat to a fairly smooth pâté.

3. Use the smoked salmon slices to line 4 lightly oiled, individual ramekin or soufflé dishes. Shred any leftover salmon and add this to the trout pâté. Spoon the pâté into the centre of each mould. Pat down firmly and chill in the freezer for 5 minutes.

4. Turn out on to individual plates and garnish with lemon and dill. Serve with melba toast if liked.

Variation: *substitute 100 g (4 oz) chopped canned water chestnuts for the cucumber.*

Microspot: *to thaw the smoked trout and salmon in the microwave cooker, place in a shallow bowl, cover and microwave on DEFROST for 5 minutes per 450 g (1 lb), turning over and rearranging the fish once during the process.*

To freeze: *not suitable for freezing.*

Far left Camembert parcels with sour cherry sauce (page 16); *Centre* Courgette drop scones with soft cheese and prawns (page 17); *Right* Garlic mushrooms (page 21)

CAMEMBERT PARCELS WITH SOUR CHERRY SAUCE

SERVES 8
PREPARATION & COOKING TIME: 30 Minutes

225 g (8 oz) frozen puff pastry, thawed
150 g (5 oz) Camembert cheese
oil for deep frying
FOR THE SAUCE:
225 g (8 oz) frozen dark cherries
1 tablespoon plum jam
1 tablespoon lemon juice
dash of soy sauce

1. On a floured board, roll out the pastry to a rectangle measuring 38×25 cm (15×10 inches). Divide into 8 equal rectangles.

2. Cut the cheese into 8 wedges and put 1 wedge on each pastry rectangle.

3. Dampen the edges of the pastry with water and bring the 4 corners of each rectangle up and over the cheese to a point, making a neat parcel. Seal the edges well and chill while you prepare the sauce.

4. Place the cherries, plum jam and lemon juice in a heavy-based saucepan and simmer until thick. Stir in soy sauce to taste and keep warm until required.

5. Heat the oil in a large saucepan or deep-fat fryer to 180-190°C (350-375°F) or until a cube of bread browns in 30 seconds. Fry the pastries until they are golden brown and puffed, then carefully remove and drain on paper towels. Transfer to individual plates and serve immediately with the cherry sauce.

Variation: *the pastries may be baked in a preheated hot oven (220°C, 425°F, Gas Mark 7) for 20-25 minutes until golden. For a smooth sauce, purée in a blender or food processor and sieve.*

Microspot: *to thaw the pastry in the microwave cooker, place it in the inner wrapper on a plate and microwave on HIGH for 1-1½ minutes; allow to STAND for 5 minutes.*

To freeze: *open-freeze until firm, then pack into polythene bags or suitable containers.*

SMOKY BACON BITES

SERVES 6
PREPARATION & COOKING TIME: 30 Minutes

225 g (8 oz) frozen puff pastry, thawed
6 rashers frozen streaky bacon, thawed
200 g (7 oz) Cheddar cheese, grated
TO GARNISH:
1 bunch watercress
50 g (2 oz) shelled walnuts, chopped
3 tablespoons French dressing

1. On a floured board, roll out the pastry to a rectangle measuring 23×30 cm (9×12 inches).

2. Using the back of a large knife, flatten each bacon slice thinly. Arrange them in a single layer over the sheet of pastry.

3. Sprinkle with cheese. Roll up the pastry from the shorter edge, Swiss-roll fashion.

4. Slice into 12 equal-sized circles. Lay them flat on 1 or 2 baking sheets, leaving space for spreading.

5. Grill under a preheated moderately hot grill until golden and bubbly. Turn the pastries over and grill the second side.

6. While the bacon bites are cooking, make the garnish. Arrange a posy of watercress on each of 6 individual plates. Divide the chopped walnuts between them and toss with French dressing. As soon as the pastries are cooked, add 2 to each plate and serve.

Variation: *use grated Red Leicester cheese instead of Cheddar.*

Microspot: *to thaw the bacon in the microwave cooker, place on a plate and microwave on DEFROST for 3 minutes, separating the rashers halfway through the process. Allow to STAND for 5 minutes.*

To freeze: *open-freeze the pastries until firm. Pack carefully into a rigid container, cover and freeze for up to 1 month. Reheat in a preheated hot oven (220°C, 425°F, Gas Mark 7) for 20-25 minutes.*

WAFFLES WITH SCRAMBLED EGG AND SMOKED HAM

SERVES 4

PREPARATION & COOKING TIME: 17 Minutes

4 frozen waffles

4 eggs, lightly beaten

25 g (1 oz) butter

salt

freshly ground black pepper

225 g (8 oz) smoked ham, cut into thin strips

1 tablespoon chopped fresh chives, to garnish

1. Grill the waffles or fry them in a little oil in a frying pan until they are golden brown on both sides. Drain and keep warm.

2. Mix the eggs, butter and seasoning in a small heavy-based saucepan. Place over gentle heat and stir constantly with a wooden spoon until the mixture begins to thicken to a creamy scramble.

3. Fold in the smoked ham and stir together gently.

4. Place each waffle on an individual plate and top with scrambled egg mixture. Garnish with chopped chives.

Variation: *stir chopped smoked salmon, flaked mackerel or prawns into the egg instead of the smoked ham.*

To freeze: *not suitable for freezing.*

COURGETTE DROP SCONES WITH SOFT CHEESE AND PRAWNS

SERVES 4

PREPARATION & COOKING TIME: 25 Minutes

100 g (4 oz) plain flour

½ teaspoon baking powder

pinch of salt

1 egg

100 ml (3 ½ fl oz) milk

75 g (6 oz) frozen courgettes, finely chopped

oil for frying

225 g (8 oz) low fat soft cheese

225 g (8 oz) frozen prawns, thawed

paprika, to garnish

1. Sift the flour, baking powder and salt together into a large bowl. Add the egg and slowly beat in the milk to make a smooth, fairly stiff batter. Press the batter through a strainer if necessary, to remove any lumps.

2. Fold in the courgettes.

3. Heat 1 tablespoon of oil in a heavy-based frying pan until it begins to sizzle. Drop tablespoonfuls of the batter into the frying pan and cook over medium heat until bubbles appear on the surface of each pancake. Turn and brown each uncooked side.

4. Remove the drop scones as they cook and wrap them in a clean tea towel to keep warm while cooking the remaining scones.

5. Mix together the cheese and prawns, sprinkle with paprika and serve with the drop scones.

Microspot: *if the scones cool down despite being wrapped in a tea towel, reheat them for a few seconds in their wrappings in the microwave cooker.*

To freeze: *the drop scones may be frozen without the topping. When cold, pack them in a rigid container, seal and freeze for up to 6 months. To serve, thaw at room temperature for 1 hour.*

SAUSAGE FRITTATA

SERVES 4-6
PREPARATION & COOKING TIME: 30 Minutes

6 tablespoons oil
225 g (8 oz) frozen onion slices, or 2 small fresh onions, sliced
2 medium potatoes, cooked, peeled and diced
225 g (8 oz) Dutch smoked sausage, sliced
175 g (6 oz) frozen peas
6 eggs, lightly beaten
salt
freshly ground black pepper
100 g (4 oz) grated Cheddar cheese
paprika

1. Heat the oil in a heavy-based 25 cm (10 inch) frying pan, add the onion and fry gently for about 8 minutes until the slices are soft and lightly golden.

2. Add the potatoes and continue to fry until they are just beginning to colour, turning them frequently but lightly with a wooden spoon or spatula.

3. Add the sausage and stir-fry for 1 minute; stir in the peas.

4. In a medium bowl, beat the eggs with seasoning to taste. Pour this mixture into the frying pan, reduce the heat and leave the omelette to cook without stirring, until the egg is just beginning to set at the edges.

5. Sprinkle the top of the omelette with grated cheese and paprika and slide the frying pan under a preheated hot grill. Leave until the top is golden and bubbly.

6. Carefully ease the egg away from the sides of the pan and slide the omelette on to a serving dish. Cut into wedges and serve hot or cold.

Microspot: *to cook the potatoes in the microwave cooker, peel and dice them and place in a bowl with 2 tablespoons water. Cover loosely with greaseproof paper and cook on HIGH for 4-5 minutes. Allow to STAND for 2 minutes.*

To freeze: *not suitable for freezing.*

HEALTH BURGER

SERVES 1
PREPARATION & COOKING TIME: 30 Minutes

1 frozen burger bun, thawed
1 frozen low fat burger
1 teaspoon oil
1 tablespoon sesame seeds
1 tablespoon low fat soft cheese
50 g (2 oz) bean-sprouts
2-3 slices cucumber
1 tablespoon dry roast nuts, chopped

1. Halve the burger bun and toast both the cut sides lightly.

2. Brush the burger with oil and dip it into the sesame seeds, pressing them firmly on to both sides of the patty. Cook under a pre-heated hot grill for about 7 minutes each side until cooked right through.

3. Spread the bottom half of the toasted bun with cheese, add the cooked burger and top with the bean-sprouts, cucumber and chopped nuts. Replace the bun lid and serve.

Variations: *try different toppings for the burger, for example, shredded lettuce, sprigs of watercress, onion rings and crisp-fried bacon, crumbled on top; or shredded red cabbage and carrot with coarsely chopped fresh parsley.*

Microspot: *to thaw the burger bun in the microwave cooker, wrap it in a paper towel and microwave for ¾-1 minute on DEFROST. Allow to STAND for 2 minutes.*

To freeze: *not suitable for freezing.*

Right Sausage frittata; *Far right* Health burger

VEGETABLE HASH

SERVES 4

PREPARATION & COOKING TIME: 30 Minutes

225 g (8 oz) frozen onion slices, or 2 small fresh onions, peeled and sliced

6 tablespoons oil

15 frozen potato croquettes

225 g (8 oz) frozen leeks, thawed and roughly chopped

225 g (8 oz) frozen broccoli, thawed and roughly chopped

salt

freshly ground black pepper

150 g (5 oz) Cheddar cheese, grated

25 g (1 oz) butter

4 eggs

1. Heat 4 tablespoons of the oil in a large heavy-based frying pan and gently fry the onion for about 5 minutes until it is just soft.

2. Add the potato croquettes and stir-fry until just soft. Break into pieces.

3. Add the leeks and broccoli and continue to fry, adding more oil as and when neces-sary, to make a flat golden pancake full of crisp vegetable pieces.

4. Sprinkle with seasoning, cover with cheese and place under a preheated moderately hot grill until golden.

5. Meanwhile melt the butter in a second frying pan and fry the eggs. Divide the vegetable mixture between 4 heated plates and top each portion with an egg.

Variations: *add slices of cooked smoked sausage or slivers of ham to the mixture. Experiment with different vegetables. Try using 450 g (1 lb) frozen Continental Mix or the equivalent weight of fresh prepared diced peppers, peas, corn, cut beans, courgettes and diced onion.*

Microspot: *if you wish to partially thaw croquettes before use, arrange them in a ring around the edge of a plate , cover and microwave on DEFROST for 2-3 minutes.*

To freeze: *the vegetables and cheese may be frozen before grilling.*

CHEESY MUSHROOM PUFFS

SERVES 4
PREPARATION & COOKING TIME: 30 Minutes

24 frozen whole mushrooms, thawed

12 cubes Caerphilly cheese

12 long cocktail sticks

FOR THE BATTER:

120 g (4 ½ oz) self-raising flour

pinch of bicarbonate of soda

pinch of salt

about 200 ml (7 fl oz) water

deep oil for frying

1. Remove the mushroom stalks if necessary and reserve for soup or stews. Sandwich two mushroom caps together around a cube of cheese. Spear through the centre with a cocktail stick to hold the mushrooms in position. Repeat with the remaining mushrooms and cheese.

2. Make the batter: sift the flour, bicarbonate of soda and salt together in a large bowl. Gradually stir in enough water to make a fairly stiff batter (about the consistency of double cream). Press the batter through a strainer if necessary, to remove any lumps.

3. Heat the oil in a large saucepan or deep-fat fryer to 180-190°C (350-375°F) or until a cube of bread browns in 30 seconds. Dip the mushroom and cheese 'sandwiches' into the batter, drain off the excess and deep fry the puffs until golden brown.

4. Carefully remove the puffs from the oil, and drain on paper towels. Remove the cocktail sticks and serve hot on individual plates, allowing 3 puffs per person.

Microspot: *to thaw the mushrooms in the microwave cooker, arrange them in a circle on a plate and microwave on DEFROST for 1 minute. Allow to STAND for 3-4 minutes.*

To freeze: *not suitable for freezing.*

FRENCH BREAD PIZZA

SERVES 1
PREPARATION & COOKING TIME: 25 Minutes

1 frozen French half baguette, thawed and baked

1 teaspoon butter

2 tablespoons tinned tomato sauce

2 rashers frozen streaky bacon, thawed, or ham slices

100 g (4 oz) frozen mushroom slices, thawed

100 g (4 oz) grated cheese

mixed herbs, to garnish

1. Slice the baguette in half lengthways and spread both cut surfaces with butter. Toast under a preheated hot grill until lightly golden.

2. Spread both slices with tomato sauce.

3. If using bacon, grill it until crisp. Chop the bacon or ham and arrange on top of the tomato mixture. Top with sliced mushrooms and sprinkle with cheese.

4. Grill until the cheese bubbles. Sprinkle with mixed herbs and serve immediately.

Variations: *add frozen corn instead of the mushrooms and salami instead of the bacon. Top with sliced Mozzarella cheese for a more traditional pizza flavour.*

Microspot: *to thaw the half baguette in the microwave cooker, wrap it loosely in a napkin and microwave on DEFROST for 2 minutes. Allow to STAND for 3 minutes, then microwave on DEFROST for 2-3 minutes more.*

To freeze: *the pizza may be frozen before grilling. Open-freeze, wrap in foil, place in polythene bag, seal and freeze for up to 1 month. Reheat from frozen in a preheated hot oven (220°C, 425°F, Gas Mark 7) for 35-40 minutes.*

GARLIC MUSHROOMS

SERVES 4
PREPARATION & COOKING TIME: 30 Minutes

450 g (1 lb) frozen whole mushrooms

75 g (3 oz) butter, melted

6 tablespoons fresh breadcrumbs

1 egg yolk

2 tablespoons frozen double cream, thawed, or fresh soured cream

1 clove garlic, crushed

2 tablespoons chopped fresh parsley

salt

freshly ground black pepper

100 g (4 oz) mature Cheddar cheese, grated

1. Arrange the mushrooms in a buttered ovenproof dish or 4 individual dishes.

2. In a bowl, mix 2 tablespoons of the melted butter with the breadcrumbs, egg yolk, cream, garlic and parsley. Season to taste and stir in the cheese.

3. Spread this thick paste over the mushrooms and dribble over the remaining butter.

4. Bake in a preheated hot oven (220°C, 425°F, Gas Mark 7) for 15 minutes or until golden. Serve with baked half baguettes to mop up the juices.

Microspot: *to melt butter in the microwave cooker, allow a few seconds on DEFROST.*

To freeze: *not suitable for freezing.*

CLUB BURGER

SERVES 1
PREPARATION & COOKING TIME: 25 Minutes

1 frozen quarter pounder burger

oil for frying

2 rashers frozen streaky bacon, thawed

50 g (2 oz) frozen onion slices, or ½ small fresh onion, peeled and sliced

1 frozen burger bun, thawed

1 tablespoon butter

1 tablespoon hamburger relish or mustard

3 slices tomato

1 large lettuce leaf

1. Brush the burger with oil and fry in a hot frying pan over a high heat for about 2 minutes on each side or until golden brown. Reduce the heat and continue to cook until the burger is cooked right through. Drain on paper towels and keep warm.

2. Add the bacon to the frying pan and fry until crisp. Drain and keep warm with the burger. Add the onion to the frying pan and stir-fry in the bacon fat for 4-5 minutes until it is soft and lightly golden.

3. Meanwhile halve the burger bun and lightly toast both cut sides under a preheated hot grill.

4. Butter both cut sides of the toasted bun lightly. Spread the bottom half with relish or mustard. Add the cooked burger, spread with more relish if liked. Top with the onion, bacon, tomato and lettuce and replace the lid, pressing it down lightly and holding it in place with a cocktail stick if necessary.

Variation: *use a chicken steaklet or cheeseburger and add tomato ketchup instead of relish.*

Microspot: *to remove the last of the ketchup from a bottle, add a little orange juice and butter and microwave without the lid on HIGH for 1-2 minutes.*

To freeze: *not suitable for freezing.*

MAIN COURSES

With a sensibly stocked freezer and store cupboard, you need never ask the question, 'What can we have for dinner?' Just turn to the recipes in this chapter, and you'll find all kinds of ideas for tempting main-meal dishes that you can have on the table in no more than half an hour.

TROUT STUFFED WITH GINGER AND SPRING ONIONS

SERVES 2
PREPARATION & COOKING TIME: 25 Minutes

2 frozen large rainbow trout, about 225 g (8 oz) each, thawed and fins removed

1 tablespoon butter

1 teaspoon finely chopped root ginger

1 clove garlic, crushed

½ bunch spring onions, cut into 4 cm (1½ inch) lengths

1 tablespoon flaked almonds

1 teaspoon soy sauce

1 tablespoon oil

about 1 tablespoon lemon juice

225 g (8 oz) frozen Oriental Mix, or the equivalent weight of fresh prepared bean-sprouts, water chestnuts, corn, sliced mushrooms, sliced red peppers, sliced beans and bamboo shoots

spring onion curls, to garnish

1. Rinse the fish and pat dry with paper towels.

2. Melt the butter in a frying pan and stir-fry the ginger and garlic over gentle heat for 30 seconds. Add the spring onions and almonds and toss together.

3. Remove the vegetable mixture from the heat and stir in the soy sauce. Spoon this mixture into the cavities in the trout and fasten the pockets with 2 wooden cocktail sticks.

4. Brush the fish with oil and fry or cook under a preheated hot grill for 4 minutes on each side until lightly golden. Remove the cocktail sticks and sprinkle the fish with lemon juice to taste. Keep warm.

5. Stir-fry the Oriental Mix vegetables according to the packet instructions and serve with the trout, garnished with spring onion curls.

Microspot: *to thaw the trout in the microwave cooker, place them head to tail on a plate and slash the skin in 2 or 3 places to prevent it from bursting. Microwave on DEFROST for 7-9 minutes, shielding the head and tail with small pieces of foil if necessary (check your handbook to make sure that it is permissable to use foil in your microwave cooker).*

To freeze: *place the stuffed uncooked fish on pieces of foil and wrap securely. Place the parcels in a polythene bag, seal and freeze for up to 1 month. Thaw at room temperature for 3-4 hours and cook as instructed.*

Top right Sesame chicken kebabs (page 25); *Centre* Chicken livers oriental (page 25); *Bottom* Trout stuffed with ginger and spring onions

---

HAKE FLORENTINE

SERVES 4
PREPARATION & COOKING TIME: 25 Minutes

2 tablespoons butter
1 clove garlic, crushed
750 g (1 ½ lb) frozen hake fillets, thawed and cubed
1 tablespoon lemon juice
salt
freshly ground black pepper
6 tablespoons dry white wine, e.g. Muscadet
500 g (1 ¼ lb) frozen creamed spinach, thawed
6-8 slices frozen garlic bread, partially thawed

1. Heat the butter and garlic gently in a frying pan and cook over low heat until the butter melts.

2. Stir in the hake and fry gently for 1 minute. Add the lemon juice, seasoning and wine. Leave over a very low heat to blend the flavours while cooking the spinach.

3. In a saucepan, gently cook the creamed spinach, stirring until thoroughly heated through. Season and spoon into a shallow heatproof dish. Spoon over the fish mixture.

4. Cover with the slices of garlic bread and place under a preheated hot grill until the topping is golden.

Microspot: *to partially thaw the garlic bread in the microwave cooker, wrap loosely in a napkin and microwave on DEFROST for 2 minutes. Allow to STAND for 3 minutes. If necessary, microwave on DEFROST for 1-2 minutes more.*

To freeze: *omit garlic bread and allow to cool. Place in a rigid container, cover and freeze for up to 3 months. Reheat in a moderate oven (180°C, 350°F, Gas Mark 4) for 2 hours. Add the topping and grill.*

SEAFOOD PASTA

SERVES 4
PREPARATION & COOKING TIME: 25 Minutes

300 g (10 oz) shell pasta
salt
FOR THE SAUCE:
2 × 170 g (6 oz) packets frozen cod in mushroom sauce
225 g (8 oz) frozen prawns, thawed
salt
freshly ground black pepper
1 tablespoon lemon juice
6 tablespoons grated Parmesan cheese

1. Cook the pasta in a saucepan of boiling salted water for 15-20 minutes or until 'al dente' or just firm to the bite.

2. Meanwhile, cook the packets of cod in sauce following the manufacturer's instructions. Snip the packets and turn the mixture into a small saucepan. Lightly flake the fish into bite-sized pieces.

3. Add the prawns to the cod, season to taste and stir in the lemon juice. Heat the sauce over gentle heat.

4. Drain the pasta and turn into a serving dish. Top with the sauce, toss and serve with the grated cheese.

Variation: *use frozen cod in cheese sauce instead of mushroom sauce, and reduce the amount of Parmesan cheese sprinkled on top.*

Microspot: *the frozen cod in mushroom sauce may be cooked in the microwave cooker; follow the instructions under Crispy cod gratin (page 13).*

To freeze: *follow the instructions under Hake Florentine (page 24), freezing for up to 1 month.*

CHICKEN LIVERS ORIENTAL

SERVES 4
PREPARATION & COOKING TIME: 28 Minutes

750 g (1 ½ lb) frozen chicken livers, thawed and trimmed

3 tablespoons dark soy sauce

3 tablespoons oil

100 g (4 oz) whole blanched almonds, roughly chopped into slivers

339 g (12 oz) can pineapple cubes, drained and juice reserved

2 teaspoons cornflour

2 tablespoons wine or cider vinegar

salt

freshly ground black pepper

spring onions, to garnish

1. Halve the chicken livers. Pour the soy sauce into a shallow bowl, add the chicken livers and stir gently to coat thoroughly.

2. Heat the oil in a large frying pan. Using a slotted spoon, remove the livers from the marinade and stir-fry over high heat for 3-4 minutes until browned on the outside but still slightly pink inside.

3. Add the almonds and drained pineapple cubes and stir-fry for 1 minute.

4. Place the cornflour in a bowl. Add the vinegar and half the pineapple juice and mix well. Pour the cornflour mixture over the chicken livers and cook over gentle heat, stirring constantly until the sauce thickens. Stir in a little more pineapple juice if the sauce is too thick, and season if liked.

Microspot: *to thaw the chicken livers, place them in their container but without the lid in the microwave cooker and microwave on DEFROST for 6-7½ minutes.*

To freeze: *follow the instructions under Hake Florentine (page 24).*

SESAME CHICKEN KEBABS

SERVES 4
PREPARATION & COOKING TIME: 30 Minutes

2 tablespoons oil

1 tablespoon dark soy sauce

350 g (12 oz) frozen boneless diced chicken breast, thawed

2 tablespoons sesame seeds

8 small tomatoes

8 frozen baby onions, thawed

FOR THE SAUCE:

120 ml (4 fl oz) thick set natural yogurt

1 tablespoon chopped fresh parsley

1 tablespoon chopped fresh mint

salt

freshly ground black pepper

1 clove garlic, crushed

1. Combine the oil and soy sauce in a shallow bowl and add the diced chicken. Toss to coat thoroughly. Spread the sesame seeds in a second bowl and add the chicken, using a slotted spoon. Press the seeds firmly on to the meat. Reserve the remaining oil and soy sauce mixture.

2. Thread the chicken, tomatoes and onions alternately on to 4 wooden kebab skewers.

3. Lay the skewers side by side in a grill pan and brush the vegetables with the reserved oil and soy sauce mixture.

4. Cook the kebabs under a preheated medium to high grill for about 5 minutes, until the sesame seeds are golden and the chicken is just tender.

5. Meanwhile, place the yogurt in a bowl and mix with the fresh herbs, seasoning and garlic. Serve with the cooked kebabs.

Microspot: *to thaw the diced chicken, spread it in a single layer in a shallow dish, cover lightly and microwave on DEFROST for 7-8 minutes, stirring once and breaking up any clumps of diced chicken with a fork.*

To freeze: *not suitable for freezing.*

BREASTS OF CHICKEN WITH BABY ONIONS

SERVES 4

PREPARATION & COOKING TIME: 25 Minutes

4 frozen part-boned chicken breast portions, thawed and boned
1 tablespoon butter
2 tablespoons oil
150 g (5 oz) frozen baby onions, thawed
1 tablespoon plain flour
200 ml (7 fl oz) boiling water
½ chicken stock cube
salt
freshly ground black pepper
3 tablespoons vermouth or brandy, optional
6 tablespoons single cream

1. Place each of the chicken breasts between 2 sheets of greaseproof paper. Beat the pieces of chicken with a rolling pin to flatten them slightly so that they cook more evenly and quickly.

2. Melt the butter in the oil in a large frying pan until the fat begins to sizzle. Add the chicken breasts in a single layer and fry over very high heat for 2-3 minutes on each side until golden brown and cooked right through.

3. Using a fish slice, transfer the chicken pieces to a hot serving dish and keep warm.

4. Add the onions to the fat remaining in the pan and stir-fry over gentle heat for 2-3 minutes.

5. Sprinkle over the flour and cook gently for 1 minute. In a jug, mix the boiling water with the stock cube. Gradually stir this stock into the flour mixture. Bring the sauce slowly to the boil, stirring all the time to keep it smooth. Season to taste.

6. Reduce the heat and simmer the sauce for 1-2 minutes. Add the vermouth or brandy, if using, and the cream and check the seasoning. Reheat gently without boiling.

7. Spoon the sauce over the chicken, or if you prefer, serve it separately.

Variation: *frozen asparagus can be used in place of the baby onions in the sauce.*

Microspot: *to thaw the chicken portions, arrange them in a circle on a dish, thin ends to the centre. Cover lightly and microwave on DEFROST for 5 minutes per 450 g (1 lb) turning portions halfway through.*

To freeze: *when cool, pack in a rigid container, seal and freeze for up to 1 month. Thaw at room temperature for 4 hours.*

Above, top Breasts of chicken with baby onions; *Bottom* Baked orange and tarragon chicken

Right Stilton steakgrills (page 28); *Far right* Devilled gammon steak with corn fritters (page 29)

BAKED ORANGE AND TARRAGON CHICKEN

SERVES 4

PREPARATION & COOKING TIME: 25 Minutes

4 frozen chicken breast steaks, thawed

1 tablespoon butter

1 tablespoon oil

1 teaspoon plain flour

150 ml (¼ pint) frozen concentrated Jaffa orange juice, thawed

2-3 tablespoons water

1 teaspoon chopped fresh tarragon or a pinch of dried tarragon

1 clove garlic, crushed

salt

freshly ground black pepper

TO GARNISH:

1 orange, peeled and cut into rings

fresh tarragon

1. Place the chicken steaks on a baking sheet and bake in a preheated very hot oven (230°C, 450°F, Gas Mark 8) for 20 minutes, turning them over after 10 minutes.

2. While the chicken steaks are cooking, melt the butter in the oil in a large frying pan until the fat begins to sizzle. Stir in the flour and cook for 1 minute more. Stir in the orange juice with the water. Add the tarragon, garlic and seasoning and slowly bring to the boil, stirring constantly until the sauce is thick and smooth.

3. Using a fish slice, transfer the chicken steaks to individual warmed plates, pour the sauce over each piece of chicken and garnish with orange and tarragon. Serve immediately.

Variation: *substitute dry white wine for the orange juice and thyme for the tarragon.*

Microspot: *to thaw the breast steaks in the microwave cooker, arrange them on a large platter, cover lightly and microwave on DEFROST for 7-8 minutes per 450 g (1 lb).*

To freeze: *follow the instructions under Breasts of chicken with baby onions (page 26).*

TROPICAL CHICKEN WITH PINEAPPLE AND GINGER

SERVES 4
PREPARATION & COOKING TIME: 20 Minutes

4 frozen part-boned chicken breast portions, thawed and boned
1 teaspoon dark soy sauce
1 tablespoon butter
1 tablespoon oil
1 teaspoon finely chopped root ginger
8 spring onions, cut into 4 cm (1 ½ inch) lengths
175 g (6 oz) canned pineapple cubes
2 tablespoons dry sherry
120 ml (4 fl oz) chicken stock
salt
freshly ground black pepper

1. Trim any fat from the chicken. Place the breasts between 2 sheets of greaseproof paper and flatten them slightly with a wooden rolling pin so that they cook more quickly and evenly.

2. Brush the chicken with soy sauce.

3. Melt the butter in the oil in a large heavy-based frying pan until the fat begins to sizzle. Add the chicken breasts in a single layer and fry over high heat for 2-3 minutes on each side until golden brown and cooked right through. Using a fish slice, transfer the chicken breasts to a serving dish and keep warm.

4. Add the ginger to the fat remaining in the frying pan and stir-fry over gentle heat for 1 minute. Stir in the onions and pineapple, the sherry, stock and seasoning.

5. Bring to the boil, reduce the heat and simmer for 1-2 minutes. Spoon the sauce over the chicken and serve.

Microspot: *to thaw the chicken in the microwave cooker, follow the instructions under Breasts of chicken with baby onions (page 26).*

To freeze: *follow the instructions under Breasts of chicken with baby onions (page 26).*

STILTON STEAKGRILLS

SERVES 2
PREPARATION & COOKING TIME: 28 Minutes

1 teaspoon oil
2 frozen steakgrills
100 g (4 oz) Stilton cheese, crumbled
2 teaspoons butter
dash of Tabasco
dash of Worcestershire sauce
1 tablespoon lemon juice
2 tablespoons brandy

1. Lightly oil a heavy-based frying pan and place over high heat. When the oil is hot, add the steakgrills and fry for 2-3 minutes until brown on both sides. Transfer them to a grill rack.

2. Top each steakgrill with crumbled cheese and pop them under a preheated hot grill to melt the cheese quickly.

3. Meanwhile, add the butter to the frying pan. Stir in the Tabasco, Worcestershire sauce and lemon juice and heat gently until the butter melts.

4. Heat the brandy in a soup ladle, ignite it and carefully add it to the sauce. Transfer the steakgrills to a serving dish and spoon the sauce around them. Serve immediately with French fried potatoes.

Variation: *the Stilton steakgrills may be served without the sauce on split, lightly toasted rolls. Add lettuce, sliced tomato and relish.*

Microspot: *to heat the brandy for flambéing in the microwave cooker, place it in a small bowl and microwave on HIGH for 15 seconds. Remove from the cooker, pour over the food and ignite.*

To freeze: *not suitable for freezing.*

LAMB CHOPS WITH GARLIC CHEESE

SERVES 4

PREPARATION & COOKING TIME: 19 Minutes

8 frozen lamb chops, thawed

4 tablespoons lemon juice

2 tablespoons oil

2 cloves garlic, crushed

1 teaspoon dried oregano

65 g (2½ oz) Boursin cheese

8 thick tomato slices

salt

freshly ground black pepper

1. Arrange the chops side by side on the rack of a grill pan.

2. In a bowl, mix the lemon juice, oil, garlic and oregano and use to brush the chops thickly.

3. Cook the chops under a preheated hot grill for about 4 minutes. Turn them over and brush with more sauce. Grill for 4 minutes more.

4. Spread the cheese thickly over each chop and top each with a slice of tomato. Dribble over the rest of the sauce and season the chops. Return to the grill until the edges of the tomato start to brown.

5. Serve with lemon rice or steamed potatoes, if liked, and a crisp green vegetable.

Variation: *use mashed Roquefort cheese instead of Boursin.*

Microspot: *to thaw the chops in the microwave cooker, arrange them on a plate, thin ends to the centre. Microwave on DEFROST for 8-9 minutes per 450 g (1 lb) turning over and rearranging once during the process.*

To freeze: *not suitable for freezing.*

DEVILLED GAMMON STEAKS WITH CORN FRITTERS

SERVES 4

PREPARATION & COOKING TIME: 30 Minutes

4 frozen gammon steaks, thawed

1 tablespoon wine or cider vinegar

2 tablespoons brown sugar

2 teaspoons made mustard

FOR THE FRITTERS:

65 g (2½ oz) plain flour

½ teaspoon baking powder

pinch of salt

pinch of cayenne pepper

1 egg

400 g (14 oz) frozen corn

3 tablespoons milk

oil for frying

1. Arrange the gammon steaks on the rack of a grill pan. In a bowl, mix the vinegar, brown sugar and mustard together. Brush this mixture thickly over each gammon steak.

2. Cook the steaks under a preheated hot grill for 3-4 minutes until lightly golden. Turn them over and brush with the rest of the sauce. Grill the second sides for 3-4 minutes until golden.

3. Transfer the steaks to a warm serving plate and keep hot.

4. Make the fritters: sift the flour, baking powder, salt and cayenne pepper into a large bowl. Add the egg and mix well.

5. Stir in the corn and enough milk to make a thick batter. Heat a little oil in a frying pan and drop in spoonfuls of the batter. Fry until the undersides of the fritters are golden then turn and cook each second side. Serve immediately, with the gammon.

Microspot: *to thaw the gammon steaks in the microwave cooker, arrange them on a plate. Cover lightly and microwave on DEFROST for 8-10 minutes, turning over and rearranging once. Allow to STAND for 15 minutes.*

To freeze: *not suitable for freezing.*

FISH STEAKS EN PAPILLOTE

SERVES 4
PREPARATION & COOKING TIME: 30 Minutes

about 1 tablespoon butter

450 g (1 lb) frozen Continental Mix, or the
equivalent weight of fresh prepared diced
peppers, peas, corn, cut beans, courgettes and
diced onion

4 × 75 g (3 oz) frozen hake steaks

4 tablespoons chopped fresh parsley, or 4
teaspoons dried parsley

2 tablespoons butter

2 tablespoons lemon juice

1 teaspoon dark soy sauce

1 clove garlic, crushed

salt

freshly ground black pepper

1. Butter four 25×25 cm (10×10 inch) squares of foil.

2. Divide the Continental Mix between the pieces of foil and top each portion with a fish steak.

3. Mix the remaining ingredients together and spoon over the 4 pieces of fish.

4. Bring the edges of the foil up and fold to seal each parcel tightly. Bake in a preheated moderate oven (180°C, 350°F, Gas Mark 4) for 25-30 minutes. Snip open the foil parcels and serve each portion of fish on a plate with its accompanying vegetables and sauce.

Microspot: *if you have plenty of fresh parsley in the garden, dry some for later use. Place 50 g (2 oz) on a cardboard plate. Cover with several paper towels and microwave on HIGH for 3-5 minutes until the parsley is dry and crumbly, rearranging halfway through the process. When cool, crush the leaves and store in an airtight jar.*

To freeze: *cool quickly and pack the foil parcels in a polythene bag. Seal and freeze for up to 1 month. To serve, heat from frozen in a preheated moderate oven (180°C, 350°F, Gas Mark 4) for 30-35 minutes.*

FLASH-FRIED BEEF WITH GREEN BEANS AND WALNUTS

SERVES 4
PREPARATION & COOKING TIME: 25 Minutes

1 tablespoon dark soy sauce

300 g (11 oz) frozen fillet or rump steak, partially
thawed and cut into thin strips

3 tablespoons oil

1 teaspoon finely chopped root ginger

6-8 spring onions, halved lengthways and cut into
4 cm (1 ½ inch) lengths

225 g (8 oz) frozen sliced green beans

100 g (4 oz) shelled walnuts, roughly chopped

salt

freshly ground black pepper

2 teaspoons cornflour

150 ml (¼ pint) beef stock

pared carrot, to garnish

1. Pour the soy sauce into a shallow bowl; add the strips of beef and toss to coat thoroughly. Drain off any excess soy sauce.

2. Heat the oil in a heavy-based frying pan until it is sizzling. Add the drained beef and the ginger and stir-fry for 1 minute until the meat is lightly browned.

3. Push the meat to one side of the frying pan. Add the spring onions and continue to

stir-fry for 3-4 minutes until they are begin-ning to soften. Add the beans and stir-fry until they are just tender. Add the walnuts.

4. Stir in the meat and season to taste.

5. In a cup, mix the cornflour with the stock. Stir into the meat mixture and bring to the boil, stirring constantly. Garnish with carrot, and serve with rice or noodles.

Note: *if the meat is partially frozen it will be easier to slice.*

Variation: *substitute frozen mixed peppers for the beans.*

Microspot: *to partially thaw the meat in the microwave cooker, place it on a plate, cover lightly and microwave on DEFROST for 2-3 minutes. Slice the meat thinly, then allow to STAND for 3 minutes.*

To freeze: *not suitable for freezing.*

Above left Nut-coated pork chops with apple and sage (page 32); *Right* Flash-fried beef with green beans and walnuts

Right Fish steaks en papillote

MINUTE STEAK WITH BURGUNDY SAUCE

SERVES 2

PREPARATION & COOKING TIME: 17 Minutes

350 g (12 oz) frozen minute steaks, thawed
1 teaspoon dark soy sauce
1 teaspoon Dijon mustard
1 tablespoon oil
1 tablespoon butter
1 teaspoon plain flour
6 tablespoons Burgundy, e.g. Beaujolais
120 ml (4 fl oz) chicken stock
salt
freshly ground black pepper

1. Brush the steaks with soy sauce and spread them sparingly with the mustard. Finally brush with a little of the oil.

2. Heat the rest of the oil with the butter in a heavy-based frying pan. When the fat is really hot, add the steaks and quickly brown on both sides. Reduce the heat and fry until they are cooked to your liking. Rare steaks will require about 1-2 minutes on each side; well-done steaks 2-3 minutes on each side.

3. Using a fish slice, transfer the steaks to a serving dish and keep warm.

4. Pour off half the fat remaining in the frying pan and sprinkle the flour over the remainder. Cook over medium heat for 1 minute then stir in the Burgundy and stock. Simmer the sauce for 3 minutes, stirring constantly and incorporating any pan scrapings into the sauce.

5. Season to taste, spoon the sauce over the steaks and serve.

Microspot: *to thaw the steaks in the microwave cooker arrange them on a plate, cover loosely and microwave on DEFROST for 3-5 minutes, turning over and rearranging once during the process.*

To freeze: *not suitable for freezing.*

NUT-COATED PORK CHOPS WITH APPLE AND SAGE

SERVES 4

PREPARATION & COOKING TIME: 17 Minutes

4 large frozen pork chops, thawed and trimmed of excess fat
paprika
100 g (4 oz) shelled walnuts, coarsely chopped
225 g (8 oz) frozen Bramley apple slices
2 fresh sage leaves, chopped
1 tablespoon lemon juice
salt
freshly ground black pepper

1. Lay the chops on the rack of a grill pan and sprinkle them lightly with paprika. Cook under a preheated very hot grill for 8-10 minutes until the meat is golden and the fat crisp.

2. Turn the chops over and sprinkle with a little more paprika. Grill for 1 minute.

3. In a bowl, mix the chopped walnuts, apple, sage and lemon juice. Season to taste. Spread the mixture thickly on top of the chops. Return to the grill until the edges of the apple start to brown slightly and the topping is hot.

4. Transfer to a hot serving plate and serve with courgettes, or steamed potatoes and mange tout peas, if liked.

Microspot: *to thaw the chops in the microwave cooker, follow the instructions for lamb chops under Lamb chops with garlic cheese (see page 29).*

To freeze: *open-freeze until firm, then wrap in film and pack into a rigid container or polythene bag. Seal and freeze for up to 3 months. Reheat from frozen in a preheated moderate oven (180°C, 350°F, Gas Mark 4) for 1 hour.*

KIDNEY, BACON AND APPLE KEBABS

SERVES 4
PREPARATION & COOKING TIME: 22 Minutes

450 g (1 lb) frozen lambs' kidneys, thawed
12 rashers frozen streaky bacon, thawed
225 g (8 oz) frozen Bramley apple slices
2 tablespoons butter, melted
1 clove garlic, crushed
1 tablespoon chopped fresh parsley
paprika

1. Cut the kidneys in half and snip away any connecting tubes or tissue.

2. Remove any small bones from the bacon and cut each rasher into half widthways.

3. Wrap 2 apple slices in each piece of bacon to make 24 rolls.

4. Thread the halved kidneys and bacon rolls alternately on to 4 wooden kebab skewers.

5. Lay the skewers side by side on the rack of a grill pan.

6. Stir the melted butter, garlic and parsley together in a small bowl, and brush thickly over each kebab. Sprinkle with paprika and cook under a preheated high grill for 5-6 minutes, turning and basting the kebabs at least once during cooking. Serve with brown rice or buttered noodles and tomato salad.

Note: *take care not to overcook the kidneys as they will become dry and tasteless.*

Microspot: *to thaw the kidneys in the microwave cooker, place them on a plate and prick lightly with a fork. Cover loosely and microwave on DEFROST for 4-5 minutes, turning and rearranging once during the process. Separate individual kidneys and allow to STAND until fully thawed.*

To freeze: *not suitable for freezing.*

FISHERMAN'S CRISP

SERVES 4
PREPARATION & COOKING TIME: 30 Minutes

4 × 170 g (6 oz) packets frozen cod in parsley sauce
225 g (8 oz) frozen corn
1 teaspoon fennel or dill seeds
2 hard-boiled eggs, peeled and halved
3 × 25 g (1 oz) packets ready salted crisps, lightly crushed
100 g (4 oz) Cheddar cheese, grated

1. Bring a saucepan of water to the boil, and add the sachets of fish. Bring the water back to the boil, reduce the heat and simmer for 15 minutes. Meanwhile, in a second pan, cook the corn in boiling salted water for 4-5 minutes. Drain well.

2. Snip one end off each packet of fish and pour the contents into a shallow, ovenproof gratin dish.

3. Lightly flake the fish and gently stir in the cooked corn, the fennel or dill seeds and the eggs. Check the seasoning.

4. Mix the crushed crisps and grated cheese together and sprinkle over the fish. Bake in a preheated moderately hot oven (190°C, 375°F, Gas Mark 5) for 10-12 minutes. Serve immediately.

Microspot: *to freshen crisps that have become soft, place in a bowl and microwave on HIGH for 10-30 seconds. Allow to STAND for 1 minute.*

To freeze: *not suitable for freezing.*

MEXICAN CHILI BEEF WITH TACOS

SERVES 4
PREPARATION & COOKING TIME: 30 Minutes

3 tablespoons oil

450 g (1 lb) frozen minced beef, thawed

1 tablespoon chili powder

1 fat clove garlic, crushed

397 g (14 oz) can chopped tomatoes

100 g (4 oz) frozen small whole mushrooms

250 g (9 oz) frozen Mexican Mix, or the equivalent weight of fresh prepared diced red and green peppers, corn and diced onion

439 g (15½ oz) can red kidney beans, drained

salt

freshly ground black pepper

FOR THE TOPPING:

4 tablespoons fresh soured cream or thick set natural yogurt

4 spring onions, roughly chopped

taco chips, to serve

1. Heat the oil in a heavy-based flameproof casserole. When it is very hot, stir in the meat and cook, stirring constantly, for 30 seconds.

2. Stir in the chili powder and garlic, and cook for a further 30 seconds, then add the tomatoes to the meat with the mushrooms and Mexican Mix. Simmer for 5 minutes.

3. Stir in the drained beans and simmer for a further 15-20 minutes until the mixture is piping hot. Season to taste.

4. Serve spooned over cooked rice, if liked, and top with spoonfuls of soured cream or yogurt and chopped spring onion. Accompany with the taco chips.

Variation: *instead of minced beef, add frozen and thawed sliced rump steak to the oil.*

Microspot: *if liked, the tacos may be heated in the microwave cooker. Place them between sheets of paper towel and microwave on HIGH for 30 seconds.*

To freeze: *follow instructions under Hake Florentine (page 24).*

TURKISH PILAFF WITH YOGURT AND CUCUMBER SAUCE

SERVES 4
PREPARATION & COOKING TIME: 30 Minutes

5 tablespoons oil

100 g (4 oz) frozen onion slices or 1 small fresh onion, peeled and sliced

1 teaspoon finely chopped root ginger

1 green pepper, cored, seeded and chopped

100 g (4 oz) dried apricots, chopped and soaked in boiling water for 5 minutes

50 g (2 oz) currants, soaked in boiling water

50 g (2 oz) almond flakes

450 g (1 lb) frozen Veg 'n Rice Mix or the equivalent weight of cooked rice with corn, diced red peppers, onions, peas and sliced mushrooms

150 ml (¼ pint) boiling water

1 chicken stock cube

salt

freshly ground black pepper

2 tablespoons chopped fresh parsley

FOR THE SAUCE:

150 ml (¼ pint) natural yogurt

6 cm (2½ inch) length of cucumber, diced

1. Heat the oil in a large frying pan, add the onion and ginger and fry over gentle heat for 1 minute. Add the green pepper and continue to stir-fry for 1 minute more.

2. Drain the apricots and the currants and add them to the frying pan with the almonds. Stir for a further minute, making sure all the ingredients are coated with oil.

3. Add the Veg 'n Rice Mix and stir the mixture well.

4. In a jug, mix the boiling water with the stock cube. Pour this over the pilaff. Simmer until the rice is tender – about 5 minutes.

5. Meanwhile make the sauce by combining the yogurt and cucumber in a small bowl or jug. Mix well.

6. When the pilaff is ready, season it well and lightly fork in the parsley. Transfer to a heated serving dish and serve immediately. Hand the sauce separately.

Microspot: *to soften the chopped dried*

apricots in the microwave cooker, heat 250 ml (8 fl oz) water in a heatproof jug on HIGH for 2-3 minutes, add the apricots and allow to STAND for 2 minutes.

To freeze: *omit the chopped fresh parsley, turn the pilaff into a rigid container, cover and freeze for up to 3 months. To serve, thaw the pilaff at room temperature for 5-6 hours. Reheat for 30 minutes in a preheated warm oven (160°C, 325°F, Gas Mark 3). Adjust the seasoning if necessary, and fork in the*

chopped fresh parsley. Make the cucumber and yogurt sauce as described above, and serve immediately with the hot pilaff.

Above, top Mexican chili beef with tacos; *Bottom* Turkish pilaff with yogurt and cucumber sauce

VEGETABLE FRITTERS

SERVES 2
PREPARATION & COOKING TIME: 30 Minutes

100 g (4 oz) frozen broccoli

100 g (4 oz) frozen whole mushrooms

75 g (3 oz) frozen broad beans

100 g (4 oz) frozen cut beans

75 g (3 oz) frozen onion slices, or ½ medium fresh onion, peeled and sliced

FOR THE BATTER:

225 g (8 oz) self-raising flour

½ teaspoon bicarbonate of soda

pinch of salt

375-400 ml (13-14 fl oz) water

oil for frying

tartare sauce to serve

1. Arrange the different vegetables in piles on a large platter.

2. Sift the flour, bicarbonate of soda and the salt into a large bowl. Gradually add the water and stir the mixture together to make a smooth batter. Strain the batter, if necessary, to remove any lumps. (A little more water may be needed if the batter is too thick but test-fry a vegetable before thinning.)

3. Heat the oil in a large saucepan or deep fat fryer to 180-190°C, (350-375°F) or until a cube of bread browns in 30 seconds.

4. Starting with the broccoli, dip batches of the vegetables in batter, drain off the excess and fry in hot oil until golden brown. Lift out, drain well on paper towels and keep hot. Continue until all vegetables are cooked.

5. Divide the vegetable fritters between 2 individual plates, giving each guest the selection of his choice. Serve immediately with tartare sauce.

Microspot: *mushrooms can be cooked most successfully in the microwave cooker. For a quick starter, fill 20 small mushrooms with pâté and arrange on a shallow dish. Sprinkle with a mixture of breadcrumbs and Parmesan cheese and microwave on HIGH for 3-4 minutes.*

To freeze: *not suitable for freezing.*

HAM, LEEK AND MUSHROOM ROLLS

SERVES 4
PREPARATION & COOKING TIME: 25 Minutes

8 thin slices ham

300 g (10 oz) frozen creamed leeks, thawed

350 g (12 oz) frozen sliced mushrooms, thawed

1 tablespoon chopped chives

salt

freshly ground black pepper

5 fl oz (¼ pint) double cream

100 g (4 oz) Cheddar cheese, grated

1. Put the creamed leeks in a saucepan together with three quarters of the mushrooms. Heat until bubbling, stirring to make sure the vegetables do not stick to the pan.

2. Stir in the chives and season to taste with salt and freshly ground black pepper.

3. Spread each slice of ham with the mixture. Roll up the slices neatly and arrange side by side in a lightly buttered ovenproof dish.

4. Cover the rolls with the remaining slices of mushroom. Pour over the cream and sprinkle with cheese. Brown under a grill, or in a hot oven for 5-7 minutes.

Microspot: *to thaw frozen creamed leeks or frozen sliced mushrooms, cover and microwave on DEFROST for 2-3 minutes.*

To freeze: *not suitable for freezing.*

MUSHROOM AND PEANUT BAKE

SERVES 4

PREPARATION & COOKING TIME: 30 Minutes

275 g (10 oz) frozen Pasta Mix, or the equivalent weight of pasta with diced tomato, courgettes, onion, red pepper, corn, herbs and spices, thawed

75 g (3 oz) unsalted peanuts, chopped

225 g (8 oz) frozen mushroom slices, thawed

100 g (4 oz) stuffed green olives, sliced

300 ml (½ pint) fresh soured cream

198 g (7 oz) can tuna in oil, drained and flaked

200 g (7 oz) Cheddar cheese, grated

1. Place the Pasta Mix in a large bowl. Add all the remaining ingredients except the cheese and mix well.

2. Stir three quarters of the grated cheese into the bowl.

3. Transfer the mixture to a baking dish, sprinkle with the remaining cheese and bake in a preheated hot oven (220°C, 425°F, Gas Mark 7) for 20 minutes. Serve immediately.

Microspot: *the bake may be cooked in the microwave cooker. Place all the frozen vegetables with the Pasta Mix in a large bowl. Add 2 tablespoons water, cover loosely and microwave on HIGH for 10 minutes, stirring occasionally. Carefully pour off the liquid in the bowl and stir in the remaining ingredients, except the cheese topping. Return to the microwave cooker and cook on MEDIUM for 4-5 minutes, stirring twice. Sprinkle with the topping and finish under a preheated grill if liked.*

To freeze: *omit the cheese topping, and freeze according to the instructions under Turkish pilaff (page 34), adding the topping at the reheating stage.*

SAVOURY CHEESE AND LEEK RING

SERVES 2

PREPARATION & COOKING TIME: 30-35 Minutes

1 teaspoon butter

250 g (9 oz) packet frozen choux pastry, thawed

100 g (4 oz) Cheddar cheese, grated

½ teaspoon cayenne pepper

FOR THE FILLING:

2 tablespoons butter

175 g (6 oz) frozen boneless diced turkey, thawed

1 teaspoon plain flour

225 g (8 oz) frozen creamed spinach, thawed

salt

freshly ground black pepper

fresh parsley sprigs, to garnish

1. Using the butter, grease a 23-25 cm (9-10 inch) tart tin or quiche dish.

2. Following the instructions on the packet, snip a 4 cm (1½ inch) tip off the choux pastry bag and pipe a circle of pastry around the inner edge of the prepared dish.

3. Bake in a preheated hot oven (220°C, 425°F, Gas Mark 7) for 15-20 minutes or until the ring is well-risen and golden brown.

4. Meanwhile, melt the butter in a frying pan and sauté the diced turkey over high heat for 7-10 minutes or until tender. Sprinkle with the flour and stir-fry for 1 minute.

5. Reduce the heat and add the creamed spinach. Cook for 4-5 minutes, stirring constantly, until the spinach is completely cooked. Season generously.

6. Spoon the filling into the choux ring and sprinkle over the cheese and cayenne pepper. Return to the oven for 5 minutes more. Garnish with parsley and serve.

Microspot: *to thaw the diced turkey, follow the instructions given for chicken under Sesame chicken kebabs (page 25) reducing the thawing time to 4-5 minutes.*

To freeze: *not suitable for freezing.*

PUDDINGS & DESSERTS

Time is so precious nowadays that most of us only make puddings as treats or for special occasions. Why not reverse this trend and treat yourself and your family with the mouth-watering recipes here? Surprisingly quick and easy to make, they'll turn every meal into a special occasion!

RASPBERRY ALMOND BOMBE

SERVES 6
PREPARATION & FREEZING TIME: 30 Minutes

1 litre (1¾ pints) raspberry ripple ice cream

50 g (2 oz) meringues

225 g (8 oz) frozen raspberries

50 g (2 oz) almond flakes, toasted

TO FINISH:

150 ml (¼ pint) frozen whipped cream

8-10 frozen raspberries, partially thawed

8-10 almond flakes, toasted

1. Line a 1.25 litre (2¼ pint) pudding basin with cling film. Place the ice cream in a large bowl and soften it slightly. Roughly break up the meringues and fork them in. Fold in the raspberries and the almonds and spoon into the prepared pudding basin.

2. Freeze for about 15 minutes or until just firm, turn the ice cream out on to a serving plate and remove the cling film.

3. Pipe cream around the base, and decorate with raspberries and almonds.

Microspot: *almonds may be toasted in the microwave cooker. Place the flakes in a single layer in a browning dish and micro-wave on HIGH for 3-4 minutes, turning over and rearranging every minute.*

To freeze: *follow the instructions under Chocolate ice cream torte (page 40).*

Below Three delicious desserts which are really easy to make but look as if they took hours! *Left* Chocolate nut gâteau; *Centre* Raspberry almond bombe; *Far right* Chocolate ice cream torte (page 40)

CHOCOLATE NUT GÂTEAU

SERVES 6
PREPARATION & FREEZING TIME: 30 Minutes

100 g (4 oz) Rice Krispies
225 g (8 oz) plain chocolate, melted
1 litre (1¾ pints) American rich chocolate ice cream
100 g (4 oz) marshmallows, roughly chopped
750 ml (1¼ pints) coffee ice cream

1. Line a 25 cm (10 inch) cake tin with cling film. Stir the Rice Krispies into the melted chocolate in a bowl and press this mixture over the base and well up the sides of the prepared cake tin. Freeze the tin for 5 minutes.

2. Spoon the chocolate ice cream into the chilled cereal-lined tin. Cover with a layer of marshmallows.

3. Top with the coffee ice cream, pressing it down firmly to fill the tin.

4. Return to the freezer for about 15 minutes. Turn out on to a serving plate and remove the lining paper.

Note: *the easiest way to chop the marshmallows is with a pair of kitchen scissors. Wet the blades first so that the marshmallows do not stick to them.*

Microspot: *to melt the chocolate in the microwave cooker, place it in a glass jug and microwave on MEDIUM for 4-6 minutes, stirring once during the process. Do not use HIGH heat – this may cause the chocolate to overheat.*

To freeze: *follow the instructions under Chocolate ice cream torte (page 40).*

HONEY VOL-AU-VENTS

SERVES 4
PREPARATION & COOKING TIME: 25 Minutes

4 frozen medium vol-au-vents

300 ml (½ pint) frozen whipping cream, partially thawed

2 tablespoons runny honey

50 g (2 oz) shelled walnuts, roughly chopped

1. Place the vol-au-vent cases on a baking sheet and bake in a preheated hot oven (220°C/425°C/Gas Mark 7) for 10-15 minutes, or until well risen and golden.

2. In a bowl, whip the cream to soft peaks. Whip the honey into the cream and use this mixture to fill the pastry cases.

3. Sprinkle the tops thickly with nuts and serve.

Microspot: *if the honey has become sugary it may be liquefied in the microwave cooker. Remove the lid from the jar and microwave on HIGH for 1 minute, stirring well.*

To freeze: *not suitable for freezing.*

CHOCOLATE ICE CREAM TORTE

SERVES 6
PREPARATION & FREEZING TIME: 30 Minutes

1 tablespoon milk

6 tablespoons brandy

16 sponge fingers

1 litre (1¾ pints) American rich chocolate ice cream

150 g (5 oz) frozen dark cherries, thawed

300 ml (½ pint) frozen whipping cream, partially thawed and whipped

mint chocolate sticks, to decorate

1. Mix the milk and brandy together in a shallow bowl. Dip 8 sponge fingers into this liquid one at a time and arrange them horizontally in 2 rows in the base of a 20×12.5 cm (8×5 inch) loaf tin.

2. Soften the ice cream slightly and spoon half into the tin. Cover with the cherries and then with the rest of the ice cream.

3. Quickly dip the rest of the sponge fingers into the milk and brandy and arrange them over the ice cream.

4. Freeze for 15-20 minutes. Cut the chocolate sticks into 2.5 cm (1 inch) lengths. Turn the cake out and decorate with whipped cream and chocolate sticks. Return to the freezer until the cake is ready to serve.

Variation: *add toasted almond flakes to the ice cream instead of a layer of cherries.*

Microspot: *to thaw the cherries in the microwave cooker, place them in a bowl and microwave on DEFROST for 2-3 minutes, stirring gently during the process. Allow to STAND for 5 minutes.*

To freeze: *freeze without the decoration. When solid, remove the torte from the tin and wrap in foil. Place in a polythene bag, seal and label. Freeze for up to 2 months. To serve, unwrap, decorate and place in the refrigerator for 20-30 minutes until the torte has softened.*

APPLE AND BLACKCURRANT CLAFOUTIS

SERVES 4
PREPARATION & COOKING TIME: 30 Minutes

450 g (1 lb) frozen Bramley apple slices, thawed

225 g (8 oz) frozen blackcurrants

3 tablespoons plain flour

3 tablespoons caster sugar

3 eggs

250 ml (8 fl oz) milk

1 tablespoon oil

caster sugar for sprinkling

1. Arrange the apple slices and blackcurrants in a buttered ovenproof shallow dish.

2. Sift the flour into a mixing bowl and stir in the sugar. Make a hollow in the centre and break in the eggs. Slowly beat them into the flour, adding the milk gradually until you have a smooth batter – or work the mixture in an electric blender or food processor.

3. Stir in the oil and pour the batter over the back of a wooden spoon on to the fruit so that the fruit is not disturbed.

4. Bake in a moderately hot oven (200°C, 400°F, Gas Mark 6) for 25 minutes or until set. Serve the Clafoutis immediately with cream or custard.

Microspot: *to thaw the apple slices in the microwave cooker, follow the instructions under Apple streusel cake (page 67).*

To freeze: *not suitable for freezing.*

RASPBERRY CROÛTES

SERVES 4
PREPARATION & COOKING TIME: 25 Minutes

4 thin slices white bread

100 g (4 oz) melted butter

brown sugar

150 ml (¼ pint) frozen whipping cream, thawed and whipped

175 g (6 oz) frozen raspberries, thawed and drained

4-6 tablespoons sugar

1. Using a 9 cm (3½ inch) cutter, stamp out 4 circles from the slices of bread.

2. Pour the melted butter into a shallow bowl. Dip each circle of bread into the butter and press into a muffin or deep tartlet tin. Sprinkle each slice with brown sugar and bake the cases in a preheated moderate oven (180°C, 350°F, Gas Mark 4) for 10-12 minutes until crisp and golden.

3. Carefully transfer the bread to a wire rack to cool slightly.

4. Put a spoonful of whipped cream into the bottom of each case, fill with the fruit and top with sugar. Add more cream if liked.

Microspot: *to thaw the raspberries in the microwave cooker, place them in a bowl, cover and microwave on DEFROST for 2-3 minutes. Allow to STAND for 3 minutes. Do not over-microwave the raspberries. They should still be slightly frosty.*

To freeze: *the completed dessert is not suitable for freezing. The croûtes are best stored in an airtight tin.*

MARBLED STRAWBERRY CREAM

SERVES 4
PREPARATION TIME: 10 Minutes

225 g (8 oz) frozen strawberries, partially thawed

150 ml (¼ pint) frozen whipping cream, partially thawed

1 litre (1¾ pints) vanilla ice cream

TO DECORATE:
whole frozen strawberries
4 sprigs of mint

1. Purée the strawberries in a blender or food processor.

2. In a medium bowl, whip the cream to soft peaks. Swirl in the strawberry purée to create a marbled effect.

3. Spoon the ice cream into 4 individual serving dishes. Carefully spoon over the strawberry cream.

4. Decorate each dessert with whole frozen strawberries and a sprig of mint.

Variation: *use frozen raspberries in place of strawberries, retaining a few for decoration; or replace the strawberries with frozen blackcurrants, lightly cooked and sweetened.*

Microspot: *to partially thaw the strawberries in the microwave cooker, place them in a bowl, cover and microwave on DEFROST for 2-3 minutes.*

To freeze: *not suitable for freezing.*

LIQUEUR FRUIT FLAN

SERVES 8

PREPARATION & COOKING TIME: 13 Minutes

1 large sponge flan case

100 g (4 oz) sugar

3 tablespoons rum

3 tablespoons water

225 g (8 oz) low fat soft cheese

2 tablespoons runny honey

pinch of ground cinnamon

1 tablespoon single cream or top of the milk

450 g (1 lb) frozen dark cherries, thawed

3 tablespoons cherry jam, warmed

1. Place the flan case on a large serving plate.

2. Mix the sugar, rum and water in a heavy-based saucepan. Place over low heat and bring to the boil, stirring constantly. Boil fiercely, without stirring, for 2-3 minutes. Pour this syrup over the flan case.

3. In a bowl, beat the cheese, honey, cinnamon and cream or milk and spread the mixture in the flan case.

4. Arrange the cherries over the cheese mixture. Glaze with warmed cherry jam.

Microspot: *to thaw the cherries in the microwave cooker, follow the instructions under Chocolate ice cream torte (page 40) thawing for 5-7 minutes.*

To freeze: *open freeze the unglazed flan, then wrap in foil and freeze for up to 2 months. Thaw at room temperature for 2-3 hours. Glaze before serving.*

STRAWBERRY YOGURT SUNDAE

SERVES 4
PREPARATION TIME: 18 Minutes

135 g (4¾ oz) packet strawberry jelly

4 tablespoons boiling water

5 tablespoons cold water

3 × 150 g (5 oz) strawberry yogurts

225 g (8 oz) frozen strawberries

150 ml (¼ pint) frozen whipping cream, partially thawed and whipped

TO DECORATE

strawberries

strawberry jam

1. Place the jelly in a bowl. Add the boiling water and stir until dissolved. Stir in the cold water and chill the jelly in the refrigerator until just beginning to set.

2. Beat the yogurt into the jelly.

3. Spoon alternate layers of strawberry yogurt mixture and frozen strawberries into 4 sundae glasses.

4. Top each one with a spoonful of cream and decorate with strawberries and jam, trickled over the cream.

Microspot: *to dissolve the jelly cubes or crystals in the microwave cooker, place the jelly in a bowl with 4 tablespoons of water and microwave on HIGH for 1-1½ minutes. Stir until dissolved, then add the cold water.*

To freeze: *not suitable for freezing.*

Below, left to right Liqueur fruit flan; Rhubarb and orange fool (page 45); Strawberry yogurt sundae

WHOLE BERRY COMPÔTE

SERVES 4

PREPARATION & COOKING TIME: 13 Minutes

2 tablespoons honey
2 tablespoons frozen orange juice
225 g (8 oz) frozen strawberries
225 g (8 oz) frozen raspberries
225 g (8 oz) frozen blackcurrants
225 g (8 oz) frozen dark cherries
3 tablespoons caster sugar (optional)
1 tablespoon Kirsch
TO SERVE
wafer thin almond biscuits or macaroons
frozen whipped cream or plain yogurt

1. Mix the honey and orange juice in a large saucepan and heat gently, stirring occasionally, until the honey has dissolved.

2. Add the frozen fruit and heat very gently for 1-2 minutes until the juices start to flow.

3. Turn the fruit into a serving bowl, sprinkle with the sugar, if needed, and allow to cool.

4. Stir in the Kirsch. Serve with biscuits and whipped cream or spoonfuls of yogurt.

Variation: *add frozen blackberries in place of blackcurrants.*

Microspot: *steps 1 and 2 may be completed in the microwave cooker. Microwave the honey and orange juice on HIGH for 30-45 seconds; add the fruit and microwave for 2-3 minutes on HIGH, stirring once during the process.*

To freeze: *place in a rigid container, seal and freeze for up to 6 months. Thaw at room temperature for 4-6 hours.*

CHOUX PUFFS WITH BLACKCURRANT SAUCE

SERVES 4

PREPARATION & COOKING TIME: 30 Minutes

250 g (9 oz) frozen choux pastry, thawed
oil for frying
2 tablespoons sifted icing sugar
225 g (8 oz) frozen blackcurrants
3 tablespoons caster sugar
crème fraîche or single cream, to serve

1. Snip a 4 cm (1½ inch) tip off the choux pastry bag.

2. Heat the oil in large saucepan or deep-fat fryer to 180-190°C (350-375°F) or until a cube of bread browns in 30 seconds.

3. Carefully drop 1 cm (½ inch) balls of choux paste into the hot fat and fry 4 or 5 at a time for 3-4 minutes until they are well puffed up and golden brown.

4. Remove the puffs with a slotted spoon and drain well on paper towels while frying the remaining choux paste. Dust the puffs with sugar, place in a dish and keep hot.

5. Combine the blackcurrants and caster sugar in a saucepan and simmer over gentle heat for 5-10 minutes. Purée in a blender or food processor, or press through a sieve. Spoon over the hot choux puffs and serve with crème fraîche or cream.

Microspot: *the blackcurrants may be cooked in the microwave cooker. Place in a large bowl with the sugar and microwave on HIGH for 2-3 minutes. Allow to STAND for 2 minutes.*

To freeze: *the puffs and sauce are best frozen separately. Open-freeze the puffs, then place in a polythene bag, and seal. Place the sauce in a rigid container and cover. Freeze both for up to 3 months. Reheat the puffs from frozen in a preheated hot oven (220°C, 425°F, Gas Mark 7) for 15-20 minutes, and gently heat the sauce in a heavy-bottomed saucepan.*

CHOCOLATE-TOPPED CHERRY CROISSANTS

SERVES 4
PREPARATION & COOKING TIME: 20 Minutes

4 croissants
450 g (1 lb) frozen dark cherries
1 teaspoon cornflour mixed to a paste with 2 tablespoons water
100 g (4 oz) chocolate, melted

1. Slice each croissant in half horizontally and lightly toast the tops under a preheated hot grill.

2. Place the cherries in a medium saucepan and bring to a gentle simmer. Stir 1 tablespoon of the hot cherry juice into the cornflour paste. Return this mixture to the cherries in the pan and continue to stir until the mixture thickens slightly.

3. Arrange the bottom halves of the croissants on 4 individual serving plates and spoon over the cherry filling. Cover with the croissant tops.

4. Dribble over the melted chocolate and serve at once.

Microspot: *to melt chocolate in the microwave cooker, follow the instructions under Chocolate nut gâteau (page 39).*

To freeze: *open freeze until firm, wrap in foil and place the croissants in a polythene bag. Seal and freeze for up to 1 month. Thaw at room temperature for 2-4 hours.*

RHUBARB AND ORANGE FOOL

SERVES 4
PREPARATION & COOKING TIME: 20 Minutes

450 g (1 lb) frozen rhubarb
75 g (3 oz) brown sugar
1 teaspoon finely grated orange rind
2 tablespoons frozen orange juice
2 teaspoons Pernod, optional
300 ml (½ pint) frozen whipping cream, partially thawed and whipped
1 teaspoon preserved ginger, thinly sliced and shredded orange rind, to decorate
small sweet biscuits, to serve

1. Place the rhubarb, sugar, finely grated orange rind and juice in a saucepan and cook over medium heat for about 5 minutes until the fruit is tender.

2. Drain thoroughly, reserving the juice for another use if liked. Purée the fruit in a blender or food processor or press through a sieve. Spoon into a bowl.

3. Stir in the Pernod, if liked, and add the whipped cream to make a thick fool.

4. Spoon into small bowls or sundae glasses and top each dessert with a little preserved ginger and shredded orange rind. Serve with small sweet biscuits.

Variations: *use frozen Bramley apples slices in place of the rhubarb; the Pernod could be replaced with rum for either rhubarb or apple fool.*

Microspot: *fresh orange rind may be dried in the microwave cooker and stored in an airtight jar until required. Place the rind on a glass plate and microwave on HIGH until brittle. Crumble before storing.*

To freeze: *cover the individual desserts in cling film, freeze and then pack in a polythene bag. Seal and freeze for up to 3 months. Thaw in the refrigerator for 2-3 hours.*

PACKED LUNCHES

Packed lunches for work or school need no longer consist of the traditional soggy sandwich, hurriedly put together last thing at night or first thing in the morning. Take your pick from these imaginative and healthy recipes and every lunchtime will be a feast of surprises!

SAUSAGE AND BAKED BEAN PASTIES

SERVES 6
PREPARATION & COOKING TIME: 30 Minutes
225 g (8 oz) frozen shortcrust pastry, thawed
100 g (4 oz) frozen skinless pork sausages, cooked and sliced
225 g (8 oz) can baked beans, lightly drained
pinch of dried mixed herbs
1 egg, lightly beaten

1. On a floured board, roll out the pastry to a rectangle measuring approximately 38 × 25cm (15×10 inches). Cut into 6 squares.

2. Combine the sausages, beans and herbs in a bowl. Divide between the squares, leaving a border of plain pastry all around. Brush the pastry edges with egg. Fold in half to make 6 triangles. Seal the edges and transfer the pasties to a baking sheet. Brush with beaten egg.

3. Bake in a preheated moderately hot oven (190°C, 375°F, Gas Mark 5) for 15-20 minutes until golden. Serve while warm.

Microspot: *to thaw the pastry in the microwave cooker, place it in its inner wrapper on a plate and microwave on HIGH for 1½-2 minutes. Allow to STAND for 5 minutes.*

To freeze: *open freeze the uncooked pasties, then pack in a rigid polythene container. To serve, place on a damp baking sheet and cook in a preheated moderately hot oven (190°C, 375°F, Gas Mark 5) for 20 minutes, then reduce the temperature to* moderate (180°C, 350°F, Gas Mark 4) and cook for 10-15 minutes more.

HAM AND PEANUT SALAD

SERVES 4
PREPARATION & COOKING TIME: 22 Minutes
1 tablespoon lemon juice
1 tablespoon water
1 red-skinned apple, cored and diced
100 g (4 oz) frozen peas
100 g (4 oz) frozen mixed sliced peppers, chopped
200 g (7 oz) cooked, lean ham, cut into bite-sized pieces
2 celery sticks, cut into bite-sized pieces
50 g (2 oz) salted peanuts
1 small lettuce, washed
FOR THE DRESSING:
3 tablespoons salad oil
2 tablespoons natural yogurt
1 tablespoon wine vinegar
½ teaspoon Dijon mustard
salt
freshly ground black pepper

1. Mix the lemon juice and water in a small bowl. Add the diced apple and toss to coat.

2. Bring a saucepan of water to the boil, add the peas and peppers and cook for 5-6 minutes until just tender. Drain, plunge into cold water and drain again.

3. Place the ham in a bowl and add the peas and peppers. Drain the apple and add it to the bowl with the celery and peanuts. Fold the ingredients all together to mix well.

4. Arrange a bed of lettuce leaves in a rigid polythene box. Top with the salad.

5. Mix all the ingredients for the dressing together in a screw top jar or polythene tumbler with tight-fitting lid. Transport separately and shake and pour over the salad just before serving.

Variation: *substitute cooked diced chicken for the ham.*

Microspot: *lemons will yield more juice if the skin is lightly pricked and the fruit warmed in the microwave cooker on HIGH for a few seconds.*

To freeze: *not suitable for freezing.*

Below, left to right Puffed pizza squares with ham (page 48); Bacon, broad bean and croûton salad; Ham and peanut salad

Above Sausage and baked bean pasties

PUFFED PIZZA SQUARES WITH HAM

SERVES 6
PREPARATION & COOKING TIME: 30 Minutes

225 g (8 oz) puff pastry, thawed
6 tablespoons tomato purée
pinch of dried mixed herbs
175 g (6 oz) sliced ham, roughly chopped
100 g (4 oz) black olives
100 g (4 oz) Cheddar cheese, grated

1. On a floured board, roll out the pastry to a rectangle measuring 30×20 cm (12×8 inches).

2. Carefully roll this up over a rolling pin and unroll on to a large baking sheet. Turn in 5 mm (¼ inch) of pastry along each edge to neaten.

3. Spread the pastry with tomato purée, leaving a border of plain pastry all round. Sprinkle with herbs.

4. Cover with the chopped ham, stud with olives and top with the grated cheese. Cut into 6 squares.

5. Bake in a preheated hot oven (220°C, 425°F, Gas Mark 7) for 15 minutes or until well risen and golden brown.

6. For a warm packed lunch, pack the squares in several layers of heavy-duty foil. Alternatively, allow them to cool completely before packing them.

Microspot: *to thaw the pastry in the microwave cooker, follow the instructions under Camembert parcels with sour cherry sauce (page 16).*

To freeze: *open freeze the uncooked squares, then pack in a rigid polythene container. To serve, place on a damp baking sheet and cook in a preheated hot oven (220°C, 425°F, Gas Mark 7) for 15 minutes, then reduce the heat to moderately hot (200°C, 400°F, Gas Mark 6) and cook for 10-15 minutes more.*

SPICED CHICKEN DRUMSTICKS

SERVES 4
PREPARATION & COOKING TIME: 25 Minutes

4 frozen chicken drumsticks, thawed
2 tablespoons oil
3 tablespoons tomato ketchup
1 tablespoon wine vinegar
2 tablespoons brown sugar
1 teaspoon made mustard
1 teaspoon Worcestershire sauce

1. Brush the chicken with oil and cook, skin side down, under a preheated medium grill for 5 minutes.

2. Meanwhile combine the remaining ingredients in a small saucepan and bring to the boil over medium heat, stirring constantly.

3. Remove the chicken from the grill and brush thickly with the sauce. Return to the grill for a further 5-10 minutes, turning and basting the drumsticks with the sauce until they are tender and cooked right through.

4. Wrap in several layers of heavy-duty foil to serve warm or allow to cool and pack in a rigid polythene box.

Microspot: *to thaw the drumsticks in the microwave cooker arrange them on a plate, radiating outwards like the spokes of a wheel, with thin ends to the centre. Microwave on DEFROST for 3-4 minutes, turning over and rearranging halfway through the process.*

To freeze: *follow instructions under Breasts of chicken with baby onions (page 26).*

BACON AND CORN BAGUETTES

SERVES 2
PREPARATION & COOKING TIME: 15 Minutes

2 frozen French half baguettes, baked
1 tablespoon butter
6 rashers frozen streaky bacon, thawed
salt
175 g (6 oz) frozen corn
2 tablespoons mayonnaise or salad cream
freshly ground black pepper

1. Slice the baguettes in half lengthways and toast the cut sides under a preheated hot grill for 1-2 minutes or until lightly browned.

2. Spread the baguettes with butter.

3. Cook the bacon under a preheated hot grill or in a frying pan until crisp. Drain on paper towels and allow to cool slightly.

4. Bring a saucepan of salted water to the boil, add the corn and cook for 2-3 minutes. Drain, plunge into cold water and drain again. Place the corn in a bowl and toss with the mayonnaise or salad cream. Season to taste.

5. Fill the baguettes with the bacon and then divide the corn mixture between them.

6. The baguettes are best served warm. Wrap them tightly in several layers of heavy-duty foil for transporting.

Microspot: *to thaw the bacon, microwave on DEFROST for 3-4 minutes, and allow to STAND for 5 minutes. Separate slices during the process.*

To freeze: *unsuitable for freezing.*

BACON, BROAD BEAN AND CROÛTON SALAD

SERVES 4
PREPARATION & COOKING TIME: 25 Minutes

8 rashers frozen smoked back bacon, thawed
salt
450 g (1 lb) frozen broad beans
1 frozen garlic bread, thawed
2-4 tablespoons oil
2 tablespoons mayonnaise

1. Cook the bacon under a preheated hot grill or in a frying pan for 4-5 minutes until lightly golden and crisp. Chop or crumble.

3. Bring a saucepan of salted water to the boil, add the beans and cook over medium heat for 4-5 minutes until tender. Drain well, plunge into cold water and drain again.

3. Slice the garlic bread and cut into small pieces. Heat the oil in a large frying pan and fry the pieces for about 5 minutes or until golden. Drain on paper towels.

4. Mix the bacon and beans in a bowl and toss with the mayonnaise.

5. Transfer to a rigid polythene box. Pack the croûtons in a separate, airtight box and add to the salad just before serving.

Variation: *add cubes of cheese or slivers of salami or ham to the salad instead of the bacon.*

Microspot: *croûtons can be made in the microwave cooker. Spread the garlic bread pieces in a single layer in a shallow dish and microwave on HIGH for 5 minutes, stirring several times.*

To freeze: *not suitable for freezing.*

SAUSAGE AND BACON TWISTS

SERVES 6
PREPARATION & COOKING TIME: 30 Minutes

6 frozen thick pork sausages, thawed

3 tablespoons sweet pickle

6 rashers frozen streaky bacon, thawed

1. Cook the sausages under a preheated hot grill for about 10 minutes, turning frequently until they are pale golden all over.

2. Spread the pickle along the top of each sausage.

3. Twist a rasher of bacon around each sausage, if necessary pinning the ends of the bacon to the sausage with wooden cocktail sticks.

4. Return to the grill, keeping the sausages close together so that the bacon cannot unwind. Turn the sausages to grill all sides of the bacon. Remove the cocktail sticks. If the sausages are to be served warm, wrap them in several layers of foil. Alternatively, allow the sausages to cool completely before packing them.

Microspot: *to thaw the sausages in the microwave cooker, arrange on a plate, radiating outwards like the spokes of a wheel. Microwave on DEFROST for 5-6 minutes, turning over and rearranging half-way through the process. Allow to STAND for 5-6 minutes. The bacon will require 3-4 minutes on DEFROST and a standing time of 5 minutes. Separate the rashers during the thawing and standing process.*

To freeze: *not suitable for freezing.*

PITTA POCKETS

SERVES 2
PREPARATION & COOKING TIME: 15 Minutes

2 wholemeal pitta breads

2 tablespoons butter

salt

150 g (5 oz) frozen corn

150 g (5 oz) Cheddar cheese, grated

1 stick celery, chopped

3 tablespoons mayonnaise

freshly ground black pepper

small bunch of watercress or cress, washed

1. Place the pitta breads under a preheated medium grill for 1 minute to 'freshen' them

2. Cut each pitta bread in half and carefully open them up. Spread the inside of the pockets with butter, and wrap in several layers of heavy duty foil to keep warm.

3. Bring a saucepan of salted water to the boil, add the corn and cook for 2 minutes until just tender. Drain, plunge into cold water and drain again.

4. Place the corn in a large bowl with the cheese, celery and mayonnaise. Mix well and season to taste. Pack in a rigid poly-thene box. Pack the watercress or cress separately. To serve, spoon the salad into the pitta bread pockets and tuck in sprigs of watercress or cress.

Variation: *for a spicy rice filling, heat a little oil in a saucepan and add 150 g (5 oz) frozen rice. Stir until the rice has thawed. Remove from the heat and stir in 1 tablespoon sultanas with mayonnaise and piccalilli to taste. Spoon into the pitta bread pockets and add shredded lettuce.*

Microspot: *to warm the pitta bread in the microwave cooker, place them on several sheets of paper towels. Do not cover Microwave on HIGH for 2 minutes, turning over halfway through the process.*

To freeze: *not suitable for freezing.*

CHEESE AND SWEET PEPPER SPREAD

SERVES 2

PREPARATION & COOKING TIME: 25 Minutes

| 2 tablespoons white wine or water |
| 150 g (5 oz) frozen mixed sliced peppers |
| 1 tablespoon oil |
| 1 teaspoon wine vinegar |
| salt |
| freshly ground black pepper |
| 1 clove garlic, crushed |
| pinch of sugar |
| 200 g (7 oz) Philadelphia cheese |

1. Heat the wine or water in a saucepan, add the mixed peppers and simmer for about 10 minutes or until tender, adding a little extra water if necessary.

2. Allow the mixture to cool slightly, then add the oil, vinegar, salt, pepper, garlic and sugar. Process in a blender or food processor or chop to a rough paste.

3. Transfer to a bowl and stir in the cheese. Season to taste.

4. Spoon the cheese into 2 individual rigid polythene containers. Serve with crackers or crudités.

Microspot: *if you soften the Philadelphia cheese in the microwave cooker it will be easier to mix. Place it on a plate and micro-wave on DEFROST for 1-1½ minutes. Allow to STAND for 30 seconds and repeat if necessary.*

To freeze: *freeze in the sealed polythene containers for up to 2 months. Thaw at room temperature for 3-4 hours.*

Below, clockwise Crumbed eggs (page 53); Cheese and sweet pepper spread; Bacon and corn scones (page 53)

CRUMBED SAUSAGE AND CHEDDAR BALLS

SERVES 4

PREPARATION & COOKING TIME: 25 Minutes

450 g (1 lb) frozen pork sausagemeat, thawed

8 × 1 cm (½ inch) cubes of Cheddar cheese

5 tablespoons dried breadcrumbs

oil for frying

1. Divide the sausagemeat into 8 equal pieces and, with wet hands, shape each one to a flat round patty. Roll each patty around a cube of cheese, sealing the joins well.

2. Place the breadcrumbs in a shallow bowl and add the sausagemeat balls. Gently shake the bowl to coat the balls in crumbs.

3. Heat a little oil in a large frying pan, add the sausage balls and fry over gentle heat for about 10 minutes until crisp and golden brown all over.

4. Drain well on paper towels. To serve warm, wrap in several layers of heavy-duty foil. Alternatively, allow to cool and pack in a rigid polythene box.

Microspot: *to thaw sausagemeat in the microwave cooker, follow the instructions under Sausage and bacon twists (page 50), increasing the thawing time to 7-8 minutes.*

To freeze: *follow freezing instructions under Breasts of chicken with baby onions (page 26).*

CHICKEN STICKS WITH COLESLAW

SERVES 2

PREPARATION & COOKING TIME: 25 Minutes

2 teaspoons soy sauce

1 tablespoon oil

1 clove garlic, crushed

1 tablespoon sherry, optional

175 g (6 oz) frozen boneless diced chicken breast, thawed

salt

freshly ground black pepper

225 g (8 oz) Classic Coleslaw Salad

1. In a shallow bowl, combine the soy sauce, oil, garlic and sherry. Mix well, add the chicken and toss to coat. Allow to stand for 5 minutes, then toss again. Drain the chicken.

2. Heat a lightly oiled, heavy-based frying pan until very hot and add the drained chicken. Stir-fry over high heat for 5 minutes until the chicken is lightly browned all over.

3 Reduce the heat and cook the chicken for about 10 minutes more or until cooked right through. Remove the chicken pieces with a slotted spoon, season to taste and allow to cool. Pack in a rigid polythene box and serve with the coleslaw.

Note: *toothpicks are a useful addition to your packed lunch box. Use them to spear the chunks of chicken.*

Microspot: *to thaw the chicken in the microwave cooker, follow the instructions under Sesame chicken kebabs (page 25) reducing the thawing time to 4-5 minutes.*

To freeze: *follow instructions under Breasts of chicken with baby onions (page 26).*

BACON AND CORN SCONES

MAKES ABOUT 12
PREPARATION & COOKING TIME: 30 Minutes

225 g (8 oz) self-raising flour

pinch of salt

40 g (1 ½ oz) butter or margarine plus 1 teaspoon
for greasing

2 rashers frozen streaky bacon, thawed

75 g (3 oz) frozen corn

1 egg

4 tablespoons milk

1. Sift the flour and salt into a large bowl and rub in the butter or margarine.

2. Cook the bacon under a preheated hot grill or in a frying pan until crisp. Crumble and stir into the flour mixture with the corn.

3. Beat the egg and milk together in a small bowl and stir enough of this mixture into the dry ingredients to make a soft dough, adding more milk if necessary.

4. Turn the dough on to a floured board and pat out to a thickness of not less than 2 cm (¾ inch). With a 4-5 cm (1½-2 inch) cutter, stamp out 12 scones, reshaping the trimmings as necessary.

5. Place the scones on a greased baking sheet and bake in a preheated hot oven (220°C, 425°F, Gas Mark 7) for 12-15 minutes. Cool on a wire rack, then split the scones, butter them and pack in a rigid polythene box.

Microspot: *to thaw the bacon in the microwave cooker, follow the instructions under Smoky bacon bites (page 16), reducing the thawing time to 45 seconds.*

To freeze: *When cool, pack the scones in a rigid polythene container and freeze for up to 2 months. To serve, reheat from frozen in a preheated moderate oven (180°C, 350°F, Gas Mark 4) for 15-20 minutes.*

CRUMBED EGGS

SERVES 4
PREPARATION & COOKING TIME: 30 Minutes

1 × 127 g (4 ½ oz) packet instant potato

100 g (4 oz) frozen smoked haddock fillets

50 g (2 oz) plain flour

pinch of ground nutmeg

1 tablespoon chopped parsley

4 hard-boiled eggs, shelled

1 egg

3 tablespoons milk

5 tablespoons dried white breadcrumbs

oil for frying

1. Make up the instant potato in a large bowl, following the manufacturer's instructions, but reducing liquid by 3 tablespoons.

2. Bring a saucepan of water to the boil, add the fish, reduce the heat and poach for 2-3 minutes. Drain, remove the skin and flake the fish.

3. Add the flaked fish, flour, nutmeg and parsley to the potato. Season to taste. Mould a quarter of the mixture around each egg.

4. Combine the egg and milk in a shallow bowl and mix well. Spread out the crumbs in a second bowl, and coat each savoury egg in egg and breadcrumbs.

5. Heat the oil in a large saucepan or deep fat fryer to 180-190°C (350-375°F) or until a cube of bread browns in 30 seconds. Deep fry the eggs, 2 at a time, in the oil for 5 minutes, then reduce the temperature slightly and cook for a further 2-3 minutes. Remove the eggs with a slotted spoon, drain on paper towels and cool. Pack in a rigid polythene box, using crumpled paper towels.

Note: *the stiffer the potato mixture the easier it is to fry the coated eggs. If possible chill them for 10-15 minutes before deep-frying.*

Microspot: *eggs should never be cooked in their shells in the microwave cooker – pressure building up inside the shell would cause them to explode.*

To freeze: *not suitable for freezing.*

MICROWAVE MAGIC

With a microwave cooker as your ally, you need never again be bothered when unexpected guests arrive or the family comes in for meals at different times. A snack for one, a nourishing family meal or a three course menu – all can be popped in the microwave to be ready in a fraction of the normal time.

CURRIED FISH SCRAMBLE

SERVES 4
PREPARATION & COOKING TIME: 28 Minutes

2 tablespoons oil
75 g (3 oz) frozen onion slices, or ½ medium fresh onion, peeled and sliced
2 cloves garlic, crushed
1 teaspoon crushed or chopped root ginger
1 teaspoon curry powder
pinch of chili powder
½ teaspoon ground turmeric
½ teaspoon ground coriander
5 ripe tomatoes, skinned and roughly chopped
6 × 75 g (3 oz) frozen cod steaks, thawed
salt
4 tablespoons natural yogurt or whipping cream
fresh coriander leaves, to garnish

1. Put the oil into a bowl with the onion, garlic, ginger, curry powder, chili powder, turmeric and coriander. Cover loosely with greaseproof paper and cook on HIGH for 3 minutes.

2. Add the tomatoes and stir well. Replace the cover and cook the mixture on HIGH for 10 minutes.

3. Cut the fish into cubes and add to the bowl.

4 Replace the cover and cook on HIGH for 5 minutes. Check the seasoning and add salt if necessary. Stir in the yogurt or cream and sprinkle with the chopped coriander.

5. Serve immediately with rice, popadoms

and sambals (side dishes) – for example, sliced bananas, sliced, layered tomatoes and onions, or cucumber raita (chopped or sliced cucumber in yogurt, with herbs).

Variation: *use frozen prawns instead of the cod and microwave on HIGH for 2-3 minutes.*

Microspot: *to thaw the cod steaks in the microwave cooker, arrange them in a circle or around the edge of a shallow dish. Cover and microwave on DEFROST for 5-8 minutes per 450 g (1 lb) turning over and rearranging during the process.*

To freeze: *omit the yogurt or cream, turn into a rigid container, cover and freeze for up to 3 months. To serve, reheat in the microwave cooker on HIGH for 5-7 minutes, stirring twice, then add the yogurt or cream.*

Right Curried fish scramble with rice, popadoms and sambals

PORK LOIN STEAKS WITH MUSTARD CREAM SAUCE

SERVES 2
PREPARATION & COOKING TIME: 19 Minutes

1 tablespoon oil

2 frozen boneless pork loin steaks, thawed

150 ml (¼ pint) dry white wine, e.g. Muscadet

FOR THE SAUCE:

1 tablespoon butter

1 tablespoon plain flour

2 teaspoons made wholegrain mustard

120 ml (4 fl oz) single cream

salt

freshly ground black pepper

3 tablespoons chopped fresh parsley

1. Put the oil into a browning dish and heat on HIGH for the maximum time recommended by the manufacturer.

2. Add the pork in a single layer and cook on HIGH for 1 minute on each side to brown slightly. Pour over the wine, cover loosely with greaseproof paper and cook on HIGH for 5-6 minutes until the pork is just cooked. With a slotted spoon, transfer the pork to a dish. Pour the juices from the browning dish into a measuring jug. Make up to 200 ml (⅓ pint) with water.

3. In a shallow dish, melt the butter on HIGH for 30 seconds. Stir in the flour and cook on HIGH for 30 seconds. Stir in the meat juice and water mixture. Microwave on HIGH for 2-3 minutes until bubbling. Beat well until smooth, add mustard and cream, season to taste and cook on HIGH for 30 seconds.

4. Spoon the sauce over the pork, sprinkle with chopped parsley and serve.

Microspot: *to thaw the pork steaks in the microwave cooker, arrange on a plate and microwave on DEFROST for 3-5 minutes per 450 g (1 lb) turning over and rearranging during the process.*

To freeze: *when cool, pack in a rigid container and freeze for up to 1 month. Thaw in the microwave cooker for 10 minutes on DEFROST, stirring twice, then reheat on HIGH for 5-10 minutes or until piping hot.*

PEPPERED STEAK AND BROCCOLI FLASH

SERVES 4
PREPARATION & COOKING TIME: 20 Minutes

1 tablespoon oil

1 tablespoon coarsely crushed black peppercorns

225 g (8 oz) frozen lean fillet or rump steak, partially thawed and cut into thin strips

1 teaspoon chopped root ginger

1 tablespoon soy sauce

4 tablespoons water

1 clove garlic, crushed

225 g (8 oz) frozen broccoli

100 g (4 oz) bean-sprouts

5 spring onions, halved lengthways and cut into 5 cm (2 inch) lengths

50 g (2 oz) almond flakes

salt

1. Mix the oil and crushed black peppercorns in a shallow bowl. Add the meat and toss to coat thoroughly.

2. In a bowl, combine the ginger, soy sauce, water and garlic. Stir in the beef mixture. Cover the bowl lightly with greaseproof paper and cook on HIGH for 2-3 minutes.

3. Stir the mixture well, add the broccoli, bean-sprouts, spring onions and almonds. Stir well, replace the cover and cook on HIGH for a further 2-3 minutes, stirring once or twice during cooking.

4. Add salt if necessary and serve with rice or noodles.

Microspot: *to partially thaw the meat in the microwave cooker, place it on a plate, cover and microwave on DEFROST for 2 minutes. Slice the meat thinly, then allow to STAND for 3 minutes.*

To freeze: *not suitable for freezing.*

GREEK LAMB

SERVES 4
PREPARATION & COOKING TIME: 25 Minutes

4 frozen lamb chump chops, thawed and trimmed of fat

2 teaspoons lemon juice

1 teaspoon soy sauce

freshly ground black pepper

1 clove garlic, crushed

100 g (4 oz) frozen Ratatouille or the equivalent weight of stewed diced tomatoes, aubergine, courgettes, red and green peppers and onions

100 g (4 oz) frozen mixed sliced peppers

FOR THE SAUCE:

2 egg yolks

1 tablespoon lemon juice

6 tablespoons hot chicken stock or water

2 tablespoons chopped fresh parsley

salt

freshly ground black pepper

1. Brush the chops on both sides with a mixture of lemon juice and soy sauce. Put them on to a large plate and season with pepper. Cover the chops loosely with greaseproof paper and cook on MEDIUM for 4 minutes.

2. Drain off the fatty juices and turn the chops over. Replace the cover and cook on MEDIUM for a further 3 minutes. Remove from the microwave cooker and allow to STAND, covered.

3. Put the garlic, Ratatouille and peppers into a medium bowl. Cover loosely with greaseproof paper, cook on HIGH for 3 minutes, stirring once during cooking.

4. In a separate bowl, beat the egg yolks and lemon juice with 2 tablespoons of the hot stock or water. Add the rest of the stock or water and cook on DEFROST for 3 minutes until the sauce thickens. Beat well, stir in the parsley and season to taste.

5. Serve the chops topped with the hot ratatouille mixture and accompanied by the sauce.

Note: *watch the sauce carefully. It must not boil or it may curdle.*

Microspot: *to thaw the lamb chops in the microwave cooker, follow the instructions under Lamb chops with garlic cheese (page 29).*

To freeze: *follow instructions under Pork loin steaks (page 56).*

PORK CHOPS WITH RED CABBAGE AND APPLE

SERVES 4
PREPARATION & COOKING TIME: 20 Minutes

1 teaspoon butter

4 large frozen pork loin chops, thawed

450 g (1 lb) frozen red cabbage with apple

salt

freshly ground black pepper

1 tablespoon red wine vinegar

150 ml (¼ pint) chicken or vegetable stock

2 tablespoons dry sherry or port

1. Using the butter, grease an oval gratin dish large enough to take the chops in a single layer.

2. Spoon half the red cabbage over the base of the dish. Arrange the pork chops on top and cover with the rest of the cabbage. Season to taste.

3. In a small bowl, mix the vinegar, stock and sherry or port together. Pour over the chops and cover loosely with greaseproof paper. Cook on HIGH for 12 minutes. Test and if necessary cook for a further 2 minutes.

Microspot: *to thaw the pork chops in the microwave cooker follow the instructions for lamb chops under Lamb chops with garlic cheese (see page 29).*

To freeze: *when cool, cover and freeze for up to 1 month. Thaw in the microwave cooker for 10 minutes on DEFROST, stirring twice, then reheat on HIGH for 5-10 minutes or until piping hot.*

MEDITERRANEAN FISH BAKE

SERVES 4

PREPARATION & COOKING TIME: 20 Minutes

100 g (4 oz) frozen onion slices or 1 small fresh onion, peeled and sliced
1 clove garlic, crushed
225 g (8 oz) frozen Ratatouille, or the equivalent weight of stewed diced tomatoes, aubergine, courgettes, red and green peppers and onions
3 tablespoons dry white wine, e.g. Muscadet
salt
freshly ground black pepper
4 × 75 g (3 oz) frozen cod steaks, thawed
1 tablespoon lemon juice
3 tablespoons chopped fresh parsley
50 g (2 oz) black olives

1. Combine the onion, garlic, Ratatouille and wine in a dish. Season to taste, cover loosely with greaseproof paper and cook on HIGH for 5 minutes or until the vegetables have softened slightly.

2. Place the fish in a shallow dish, sprinkle with lemon juice and spoon over the vegetable mixture. Cover loosely with greaseproof paper and cook on MEDIUM for 4 minutes.

3. Sprinkle with parsley and olives and serve.

Variation: _use 2 tablespoons chopped fresh fennel in place of the parsley._

Microspot: _to thaw the fish in the microwave cooker, follow the instructions under Curried fish scramble (page 54)._

To freeze: _when cool, cover and freeze without the parsley and olive topping for up to 1 month. To serve, reheat in the microwave cooker on HIGH for 5-7 minutes, stirring twice during the process. Top with olives and parsley and serve._

Above left Mediterranean fish bake; _Above right_ Coriander spare ribs

CORIANDER SPARE RIBS

SERVES 2

PREPARATION & COOKING TIME: 30 Minutes

450 g (1 lb) frozen pork spare ribs, thawed
250 ml (8 fl oz) hot water
3 lemon slices
25 g (1 oz) frozen onion slices or ¼ small fresh onion, peeled and sliced
FOR THE SAUCE:
2 tablespoons fruit chutney
1 tablespoon vinegar
1 tablespoon brown sugar
1 tablespoon lemon juice
1 teaspoon made mustard
2 tablespoons tomato purée
1 teaspoon soy sauce
2 teaspoons coarsely crushed coriander seeds

1. Place the ribs bone side up in a large dish. Add the water, lemon slices and onion. Cover loosely with greaseproof paper and cook on MEDIUM for 18-20 minutes until just tender.

2. Drain off the excess cooking juices and reserve 100 ml (3½ fl oz) in a medium jug. Add all the sauce ingredients, mix well and pour over the ribs. Cover loosely with greaseproof paper and cook on MEDIUM for 5 minutes, turning the ribs once.

Microspot: *to thaw the spare ribs in the microwave cooker, place them on a plate, thinner ends to the centre, cover and microwave on DEFROST for 5-6 minutes, turning over and rearranging once during the process. Allow to stand for 10 minutes.*

To freeze: *follow the instructions under Pork chops with red cabbage and apple (page 57).*

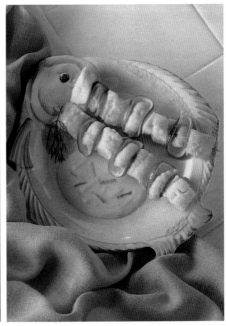

Right Smoky haddock kebabs (page 60)

SMOKY HADDOCK KEBABS

SERVES 4
PREPARATION & COOKING TIME: 20 Minutes

225 g (8 oz) frozen smoked haddock cutlets, thawed and cut into bite-sized pieces

4× 75 g (3 oz) frozen cod fillets, thawed, skinned and cut into bite-sized pieces

100 g (4 oz) scampi, prawns or mussels

2 limes, cut into thin slices

FOR THE SAUCE:

1 tablespoon soft butter

1 tablespoon plain flour

150 ml (¼ pint) dry white wine, e.g. Laski Riesling

2 tablespoons single cream

50 g (2 oz) frozen Ocean Stix, thawed and flaked

salt

freshly ground black pepper

1. Thread the smoked haddock, cod, and either scampi, prawns or mussels wrapped in slices of lime alternately on to wooden skewers and arrange them side by side in a shallow dish. Cover loosely with greaseproof paper. Cook on HIGH for 1½ minutes, then rearrange the skewers in the dish. Replace the cover and cook on HIGH for a further 2 minutes. Pour off any juices and reserve them. Allow the kebabs to STAND, covered, while you make the sauce.

2. In a medium bowl, beat the butter with the flour and stir in the wine and cream. Cover and cook on HIGH for 5 minutes. Stir well, add the flaked Ocean Stix and seasoning and cook on HIGH for 1 minute. If the sauce is too thick, add some of the reserved fish juices to correct the consistency and reheat on HIGH for 1 minute. Serve with kebabs, handing the sauce separately.

Microspot: *to thaw the Ocean Stix place them in a single layer on a plate, cover and microwave on DEFROST for 2 minutes, rearranging them halfway through the process.*

To freeze: *not suitable for freezing.*

CROISSANTS WITH SPINACH, CHEDDAR AND WALNUT FILLING

SERVES 2
PREPARATION & COOKING TIME: 11 Minutes

2 croissants

225 g (8 oz) frozen chopped spinach, thawed

1 teaspoon butter

salt

freshly ground black pepper

150 g (5 oz) Cheddar cheese, thinly sliced

75 g (3 oz) shelled walnuts, roughly chopped

1. Slice the croissants in half lengthways.

2. Put the spinach and butter into a bowl. Season to taste, cover loosely with grease-proof paper and cook on HIGH for 3 minutes. Drain off all the liquid, and stir in half the cheese and all the walnuts.

3. Spoon this mixture into the croissants and microwave between paper towels on HIGH for 1 minute.

4. Remove the croissants from the cooker and place on a plate. Sprinkle with the rest of the cheese and microwave on HIGH for a further 1-1½ minutes until the croissants are piping hot and the cheese has melted.

Microspot: *to thaw the spinach in the microwave cooker, place it in a bowl, cover and microwave on DEFROST for 2-3 minutes, turning over and breaking up during the process.*

To freeze: *omit cheese topping. Open-freeze until firm, wrap in foil and place the croissants in a polythene bag. Seal and freeze for up to 1 month. To thaw, microwave on DEFROST for 10 minutes, then sprinkle with cheese and microwave on HIGH for 3-4 minutes.*

DRY-FRIED CURRIED CHICKEN WITH SPINACH

SERVES 4
PREPARATION & COOKING TIME: 22 Minutes

450 g (1 lb) frozen leaf spinach

150 g (5 oz) frozen onion slices or 1 medium fresh onion, peeled and sliced

1 tablespoon water

2 cloves garlic, crushed

1 teaspoon grated fresh root ginger

2 teaspoons curry powder

4 frozen chicken breasts, thawed and boned

2 teaspoons gravy powder

4 tablespoons thick set natural yogurt

1. Put the spinach, onion, water, garlic and ginger into a bowl. Cover loosely with greaseproof paper and cook on HIGH for 5-6 minutes. Stir, add the curry powder and mix well.

2. Replace the cover and cook on HIGH for a further 3-4 minutes until the vegetables are just tender, stirring once during cooking. Allow to STAND while cooking the meat.

3. Cut the chicken breasts into thin strips. Sprinkle the gravy powder in a shallow bowl, add the meat and toss to coat thoroughly. Shake off excess powder. Arrange the slices in a single layer on a plate. Cover loosely with greaseproof paper and cook on HIGH for 30 seconds. Stir and cook on HIGH for a further 10 seconds. Add the chicken to the spinach and mix well. Cover and cook on HIGH for 1 minute.

4. Check the seasoning and serve each portion topped with a spoonful of yogurt.

Microspot: *to defrost the chicken in the microwave cooker, place it on a plate, cover and microwave on DEFROST for 2-4 minutes; turn the portions and microwave on DEFROST for a further 2 minutes.*

To freeze: *follow the instructions under Pork chops with red cabbage and apple (page 57).*

TROUT WITH HERBED BUTTER SAUCE

SERVES 2
PREPARATION & COOKING TIME: 16 Minutes

2 frozen large rainbow trout, thawed

1 tablespoon lemon juice

salt

freshly ground black pepper

FOR THE SAUCE:

4 tablespoons lemon juice

120 g (4½ oz) butter, cut into pieces

pinch of salt

1 tablespoon chopped fresh tarragon

1. Arrange the fish, head to tail, on a dish. Pour over the lemon juice and season.

2. Cover loosely with greaseproof paper and cook on MEDIUM for 7-8 minutes or until the fish flakes easily when tested with a fork. Remove from the microwave cooker and allow to STAND, covered.

3. Put the lemon juice into a small bowl and cook on HIGH for 30-40 seconds until the juice is bubbling. Remove from the microwave cooker and whisk in one third of the butter.

4. Cook again on HIGH for 30-40 seconds, then whisk in another third of the butter. Cook on HIGH for 30-40 seconds and finally whisk in the remaining butter. Season and stir in the tarragon. Serve immediately, with the trout.

Microspot: *to thaw the trout in the microwave cooker, follow the instructions under Trout stuffed with ginger and spring onions (page 22).*

To freeze: *the sauce may be frozen. Pack into a rigid container, cover and freeze for up to 3 months. Thaw in the microwave on DEFROST for a few seconds.*

greaseproof paper and cook the mixture on HIGH for 6 minutes.

2. Add the mushrooms, replace the cover and cook on HIGH for 1 minute. Allow to STAND.

3. Heat a browning dish for 5-6 minutes on HIGH. Add the sliced sausages and cook on HIGH for 30 seconds. Stir into the rice mixture.

4. Reheat the browning dish and cook the bacon on HIGH for 3-4 minutes. Drain on paper towels and crumble it over the rice and sausage mixture. Season to taste and serve the risotto with grated Parmesan cheese.

Variation: *omit the sausage and bacon and stir in 225 g (8 oz) frozen prawns while cooking the vegetables and rice.*

Microspot: *to thaw the bacon in the microwave cooker, follow the instructions under Smoky bacon bites (page 16), reducing the thawing time to 1-1½ minutes.*

To freeze: *pack in a rigid container and freeze for up to 3 months. Thaw in the microwave cooker on DEFROST for 10 minutes, stirring twice, then heat on HIGH for 5-10 minutes.*

SAUSAGE RISOTTO

SERVES 4
PREPARATION & COOKING TIME: 26 Minutes

450 g (1 lb) frozen Veg 'n Rice Mix, or the equivalent weight of cooked rice with corn, diced red peppers, onions, peas and sliced mushrooms

2 cloves garlic, crushed

1 teaspoon finely chopped root ginger

175 g (6 oz) frozen mushroom slices

4 frozen thick pork sausages, thawed, cooked and sliced

4 rashers frozen streaky bacon, thawed

salt

freshly ground black pepper

3 tablespoons grated Parmesan cheese

1. Put the Veg 'n Rice Mix, garlic, and ginger into a bowl. Cover the bowl loosely with

Above left Sausage risotto

Right Boston baked beans (page 64); *Far right* Mango halibut

MANGO HALIBUT

SERVES 4

PREPARATION & COOKING TIME: 12 Minutes

1 pack halibut fillets
3 tablespoons mango chutney
2 bananas, peeled and sliced
120 ml (4 fl oz) fresh lemon juice
2 tablespoons melted butter
1 tablespoon soy sauce
slice lemon or lime, to garnish

1. Cut the larger halibut fillets in half, and arrange the pieces of fish in a single layer in a shallow dish.

2. In a small bowl combine the mango chutney and bananas. Stir well and spoon over the fish, making sure the pieces are evenly covered.

3. Mix the lemon juice with the melted butter and soy sauce in a small jug and dribble evenly over the chutney-covered fish pieces.

4. Cover the dish loosely with greaseproof paper and microwave on HIGH for 5-7 minutes, depending on the thickness of the fish fillets. Serve immediately, garnished with lemon or lime.

Microspot: *to melt the butter in the microwave cooker, place it in a small bowl and microwave on HIGH for 15-30 seconds.*

To freeze: *follow the instructions under Curried fish scramble (page 54).*

BOSTON BAKED BEANS

SERVES 4
PREPARATION & COOKING TIME: 30 Minutes

1 tablespoon oil
3 rashers frozen streaky bacon, thawed and chopped
200 g (7 oz) frozen onion slices or 1 large fresh onion, peeled and sliced
1 tablespoon wine vinegar
1 tablespoon brown sugar
1 teaspoon made mustard
225 g (8 oz) Dutch smoked sausage, sliced into rings
439 g (15½ oz) can red kidney beans, drained
567 g (20 oz) can baked beans
2 tablespoons tomato purée
FOR THE TOPPING:
100 g (4 oz) fresh breadcrumbs
100 g (4 oz) Cheddar cheese, grated

1. Put the oil, bacon and onion into a bowl. Cover loosely with greaseproof paper and cook on HIGH for 5 minutes or until the onion is tender.

2. Add the vinegar, sugar, mustard and smoked sausage, stir well, replace the cover and cook on HIGH for 30 seconds.

3. Add the drained kidney beans, the baked beans with their sauce and the tomato purée. Replace the cover and cook on HIGH for 5 minutes, stirring halfway through the cooking time.

4. In a bowl, mix together the breadcrumbs and the cheese and sprinkle over the bean mixture. Brown under a preheated hot grill for 2-3 minutes.

Variation: *use diced cooked chicken or sliced hot dog sausages or cooked American frankfurters instead of the smoked sausage.*

Microspot: *to thaw the bacon in the microwave cooker, follow the instructions under Smoky bacon bites (page 16) reducing the time to 1 minute.*

To freeze: *when cool, wrap, seal and freeze for up to 6 weeks. Thaw in the microwave*

cooker for 8-10 minutes on DEFROST, stirring twice, then reheat on HIGH for 5-10 minutes or until piping hot.

INDIVIDUAL BEEF AND HERB RAMEKINS

SERVES 4
PREPARATION & COOKING TIME: 20 Minutes

1 teaspoon oil
4 sprigs fresh parsley
100 g (4 oz) frozen onion slices or 1 small fresh onion, peeled and sliced
450 g (1 lb) frozen minced beef steak, thawed
1 teaspoon soy sauce
100 g (4 oz) butter, softened
1 clove garlic, crushed
2 tablespoons chopped mixed fresh herbs

1. Lightly grease 4 heatproof ramekins. Put a sprig of parsley in each.

2. Finely chop the onion and mix with the beef and soy sauce. Reserve half the mixture and divide the remainder between the ramekins.

3. Combine the butter, garlic and chopped herbs in a bowl, and add a quarter of the mixture to each ramekin. Cover with the remaining beef mixture, pressing down gently and smoothing the tops.

4. Microwave uncovered on HIGH for 5 minutes. Allow to STAND for 2-3 minutes. Invert on to individual plates, pouring the cooking juices over each portion. Serve immediately.

Microspot: *to thaw the minced beef in the microwave cooker, place it in a shallow dish, cover loosely with greaseproof paper and microwave on DEFROST for 7-8 minutes, breaking it up with a fork at least twice and removing the meat as it thaws.*

To freeze: *cool quickly, then freeze in the ramekins. When solid, remove from the dishes and wrap individually in foil. Seal in a polythene bag and freeze for up to 2 months. To serve, unwrap, return to the ramekins and thaw for 2-3 hours at room temperature.*

Reheat, lightly covered, in the microwave on HIGH for 2-3 minutes.

SALMON STEAKS WITH QUICK HOLLANDAISE SAUCE

SERVES 4
PREPARATION & COOKING TIME: 20 Minutes

4 frozen salmon steaks, about 175 g (6 oz) each, thawed
2 tablespoons butter
2 tablespoons lemon juice
salt
freshly ground black pepper
4 lettuce leaves
FOR THE SAUCE:
100 g (4 oz) butter
2 egg yolks
pinch of mustard powder
1 tablespoon lemon juice

1. Arrange the salmon steaks in a shallow dish, thin ends to the centre.

2. In a small bowl, cook the butter on HIGH for 30 seconds, stir in the lemon juice and pour over the salmon. Season to taste. Cover each steak with a lettuce leaf. Cover the dish loosely with greaseproof paper. Cook on HIGH for 5 minutes. Allow the fish to STAND.

3. Put the butter into a small dish and cook on HIGH for 3 minutes until hot and bubbling. Place the egg yolks, mustard and lemon juice in a blender and process briefly. Gradually add the hot butter, pouring it through the hole in the lid while the machine is in operation. Mix until the sauce is thick and creamy. Season to taste. Serve in a sauceboat with the salmon.

Microspot: *to thaw the salmon steaks in the microwave cooker, arrange them in a circle round the edge of a shallow dish. Cover loosely and microwave on DEFROST for 5-8 minutes per 450 g (1 lb), turning over and rearranging once during the process.*

To freeze: *not suitable for freezing.*

SAUSAGE AND CELERY PASTA BAKE

SERVES 4
PREPARATION & COOKING TIME: 29 Minutes

225 g (8 oz) macaroni
1.2 litres (2 pints) boiling water
225 g (8 oz) frozen thick pork sausages, thawed
175 g (6 oz) frozen creamed leeks, thawed
295 g (10.4 oz) can condensed cream of celery soup
salt
freshly ground black pepper
175 g (6 oz) Cheddar cheese, grated

1. Spread the macaroni in a large shallow heatproof dish and cover with the boiling water. Microwave on HIGH for 15 minutes, stirring halfway through the cooking time. Drain and place in a large bowl.

2. Prick the sausages and arrange on a plate, radiating outwards like the spokes of a wheel. Cover with a paper towel. Microwave on HIGH, allowing 1 minute for each sausage, turning and rearranging halfway through the process. Cool slightly, then cut the sausages into slices and add to the macaroni.

3. Place the creamed leeks in a bowl, cover loosely with greaseproof paper and microwave on HIGH for 3 minutes.

4. Stir the leeks into the macaroni and sausage mixture with the soup. Mix well, season to taste and stir in half the cheese. Spoon into a 1.2 litre (2 pint) dish. Sprinkle with the rest of the cheese and microwave on HIGH for 4 minutes or until the cheese has melted. Allow to STAND for 2 minutes, then serve.

Microspot: *to thaw the sausages in the microwave cooker, follow the instructions under Sausage and bacon twists (page 50), reducing the thawing time to 3-4 minutes.*

To freeze: *not suitable for freezing.*

POPPY SEED AND MUSHROOM TART

SERVES 4

PREPARATION & COOKING TIME: 30 Minutes

150 g (5 oz) butter or margarine
2 tablespoons iced water
225 g (8 oz) plain flour
25 g (1 oz) poppy seeds
pinch of salt
1 teaspoon soy sauce
750 g (1½ lb) frozen whole mushrooms, thawed
2 cloves garlic, crushed
1 tablespoon chopped fresh lovage or parsley
1 tablespoon brandy
6 tablespoons single cream or natural yogurt
1 teaspoon cornflour
½ teaspoon butter
salt
freshly ground black pepper
chopped parsley, to garnish

1. Combine the butter and water in a bowl and beat in one third of the flour. When soft and well blended, add the remaining flour, poppy seeds and salt and mix to a dough. Using one hand, knead the pastry into a ball.

2. On a floured board, roll out the pastry to fit a 23 cm (9 inch) flan dish. Press the pastry well into the sides and neaten the top.

3. Brush the pastry case lightly with the soy sauce. Microwave on HIGH for 10-12 minutes or until puffy and cooked through.

4. Put the mushrooms into a large bowl. Cover loosely and cook on HIGH for 4 minutes, stirring after 2 minutes. Carefully drain off the excess liquid. Add the garlic, chopped herbs and brandy. Re-cover and microwave on HIGH for 2 minutes.

5. In a small bowl, combine the cream, cornflour and butter. Mix well, stir into the mushroom mixture and microwave uncovered on HIGH for 2 minutes. Season to taste.

6. Spoon the mushroom mixture into the pastry case, garnish with parsley and serve immediately.

To **freeze**: *not suitable for freezing.*

Left Poppy seed and mushroom tart

APPLE STREUSEL CAKE

SERVES 8

PREPARATION & COOKING TIME: 28 Minutes

150 g (5 oz) sugar

75 g (3 oz) butter or margarine

½ teaspoon vanilla essence

1 egg

120 ml (4 fl oz) milk

185 g (6½ oz) self-raising flour

pinch of salt

250 g (9 oz) frozen Bramley apple slices, thawed

FOR THE TOPPING:

100 g (4 oz) brown sugar

2 tablespoons plain flour

2 teaspoons ground cinnamon

2 tablespoons butter, melted

50 g (2 oz) shelled walnuts, chopped

1. Beat the sugar, butter or margarine and vanilla essence in a large bowl until light and fluffy. Beat in the egg.

2. Stir in the milk. Sift the dry ingredients and fold them into the mixture. Beat until smooth.

3. Spread half this sponge into a greased 23 cm (9 inch) baking dish. Cover with half the apple.

4. Combine the topping ingredients in a bowl and spoon half the mixture roughly over the apple layer. Repeat the layers of sponge, apples and streusel topping.

5. Bake on HIGH for 8-9 minutes, turning the dish every 3 minutes if necessary. Allow to STAND for 10 minutes before serving.

Microspot: *to thaw the apple slices in the microwave cooker, place them in a bowl, cover and microwave for 5-6 minutes on DEFROST, stirring once during the process. Allow to STAND for 5 minutes.*

To freeze: *when cool, cover, wrap and freeze for up to 3 months. To serve, unwrap and cover with paper towels. Thaw in the microwave cooker on DEFROST for 5 minutes and allow to STAND.*

Above left Apple streusel cake; *Right* Carrot cake (page 68)

CHOCOLATE AND ORANGE MOUSSE

SERVES 4
PREPARATION & COOKING TIME: 13 Minutes

120 g (4½ oz) plain dark chocolate

4 teaspoons frozen concentrated Jaffa orange juice, thawed

4 eggs, separated

150 ml (¼ pint) frozen whipping or double cream, thawed and whipped

1. Break the chocolate into pieces and place in a bowl. Cook on HIGH for 3 minutes or until the chocolate has melted.

2. Stir in the orange juice and beat in the egg yolks. Set aside.

3. In a second bowl, beat the egg whites to stiff peaks and fold them into the mousse. Spoon into individual glass dishes or ramekins.

4. Top with whipped cream and serve.

Microspot: *to melt the chocolate in the microwave cooker, follow the instructions under Chocolate nut gâteau (page 39), reducing the time to 2 minutes.*

To freeze: *freeze without the whipped cream. Cover the ramekins, seal and freeze for up to 3 months. To serve, thaw overnight in the refrigerator.*

CARROT CAKE

SERVES 8
PREPARATION & COOKING TIME: 29 Minutes

185 g (6½ oz) plain flour

2 teaspoons ground cinnamon

1½ teaspoons bicarbonate of soda

1 teaspoon ground nutmeg

pinch of salt

250 g (9 oz) frozen carrot, very finely chopped

300 g (10 oz) soft brown sugar

250 ml (8 fl oz) oil

100 g (4 oz) shelled walnuts, chopped

3 eggs, beaten

FOR THE ICING:

200 g (7 oz) Philadelphia cheese

100 g (4 oz) butter, at room temperature

1 teaspoon vanilla essence

400 g (14 oz) icing sugar, sifted

walnut halves, to decorate

1. Sift the flour, cinnamon, bicarbonate of soda, nutmeg and salt into a bowl. Set aside.

2. In a second, larger, bowl, combine the chopped carrot, sugar, oil, walnuts and eggs. Mix well. Add the sifted dry ingredients and beat the mixture until well mixed.

3. Turn the cake mixture into a deep, greased 25 cm (10 inch) ring mould. Set the dish on an inverted saucer and cook on HIGH for 12-14 minutes. The cake should shrink away slightly from the edges of the mould. If necessary cook for 1 minute more. Turn the dish during cooking if the cake appears to be rising unevenly.

4. Allow the cake to cool slightly and turn out on to a wire rack.

5. In a small bowl, beat the cheese and butter until smooth. Add the vanilla essence and beat again.

6. Gradually add the sifted icing sugar, beating well to a spreading consistency. Spread over the cake. Decorate with walnut halves and serve.

Microspot: *to soften the Philadelphia cheese and make it more manageable, follow the instructions under Cheese and sweet pepper spread (page 51).*

To freeze: *when cold, wrap the cake (without icing) in foil. Overwrap, seal, and freeze for up to 3 months. To thaw in the microwave cooker, unwrap, place between paper towels and microwave on DEFROST for 4-5 minutes. Allow to STAND to complete the process.*

CHOCOLATE CHERRY UPSIDE-DOWN PUDDING

SERVES 4-6
PREPARATION & COOKING TIME: 22 Minutes

100 g (4 oz) butter
100 g (4 oz) caster sugar
2 eggs, beaten
50 g (2 oz) cocoa powder
50 g (2 oz) dessert chocolate
100 g (4 oz) self-raising flour
FOR THE TOPPING:
25 g (1 oz) butter
25 g (1 oz) soft brown sugar
319 g (11 oz) frozen dark cherries, thawed and halved

1. Grease the base and sides of an 18 cm (7 inch) diameter soufflé dish.

2. To make the topping, dot the butter over the base of the soufflé dish and sprinkle with the sugar in an even layer. Cook on HIGH for 1 minute 10 seconds until the sugar and butter have melted together.

3. Spread the cherries over the butter and sugar mixture, reserving a few for decoration. Set the topping aside.

4. Sift the flour and cocoa powder together. Soften the butter or margarine on DEFROST for several seconds, then beat with the caster sugar until light and fluffy, and beat in the eggs.

5. Melt the dessert chocolate with 1 teaspoon water on HIGH for 2 minutes, then stir into the cake mixture.

6. Fold in the flour and cocoa powder, spoon the mixture over the topping and cook on HIGH for 7 minutes.

7. Leave the pudding to STAND for 3 minutes before turning out. Decorate with the reserved cherries and serve with whipped cream.

To freeze: *follow the instructions under Carrot cake (page 68), adding reserved cherries before serving.*

BLACKCURRANT MERINGUE PILLOWS

SERVES 8
PREPARATION & COOKING TIME: 30 Minutes

1 small egg white
250 g (9 oz) icing sugar
225 g (8 oz) frozen blackcurrants
1 tablespoon brandy
1-2 tablespoons caster sugar
300 ml (½ pint) frozen double or whipping cream, thawed

1. Place the egg white in a small bowl. Sift the icing sugar and stir it into the egg white with a wooden spoon to make a fondant mixture that is dry enough to roll out or shape.

2. Place the fondant meringue on a board sprinkled with icing sugar and roll to a thickness of 1 cm (½ inch). Using a 4 cm (1½ inch) cutter, cut out 16 rounds, rerolling the fondant as necessary. Arrange half the rounds in a wide circle on a sheet of greaseproof paper.

3. Microwave on HIGH for 1½ minutes (see Microspot). Carefully transfer the meringues to a cooling rack. Cook the remaining meringue rounds in the same way.

4. Put the blackcurrants into a small bowl. Cover loosely with greaseproof paper and microwave on HIGH for 2 minutes. Mash with a fork and press through a sieve into a clean bowl. Stir in the brandy and caster sugar to taste.

5. In a large jug or bowl, whip the cream to stiff peaks. Arrange the meringue pillows on a large serving tray or platter, top each with a spoonful or piped rosette of cream, then drizzle over the blackcurrant sauce. Serve immediately.

Microspot: *when cooking the meringues in the microwave cooker, leave plenty of room between each, as they expand considerably. Do not open the door while they are cooking, or they will collapse.*

To freeze: *not suitable for freezing.*

MENUS FOR ENTERTAINING

Even with a job and a home to run, it is still possible to enjoy the pleasures of entertaining. The trick lies in being realistic about what you can achieve in the time you have. Don't be over-ambitious – easy-to-prepare dishes like these will delight your guests *and* give you time to make the most of their company.

MENU 1

Avocados with smoked fish

Pork and apple en croûte

Layered berry and ice cream cups

AVOCADOS WITH SMOKED FISH

SERVES 6
PREPARATION & COOKING TIME: 30 Minutes

3 ripe avocados
2 tablespoons lemon juice
200 g (7 oz) frozen kipper fillets
50 g (2 oz) butter
50 g (2 oz) plain flour
250 ml (8 fl oz) milk
salt
freshly ground black pepper
1 tablespoon grated Parmesan cheese
6 tablespoons fresh white breadcrumbs

1. Halve the avocados and remove the stones.

2. Enlarge the cavities, leaving enough avocado flesh to keep the shells firm. Cut the scooped-out avocado flesh into cubes and place in a bowl. Sprinkle both the shells and the cubes with the lemon juice.

3. Cook the kippers according to the manu-

facturer's instructions. Remove any skin and bones and flake the fish into bite-sized pieces.

4. Melt the butter in a medium saucepan, stir in the flour and cook for 1 minute. Slowly stir in the milk and bring to the boil, stirring all the time to make a smooth sauce.

5. Remove from the heat and fold in the avocado cubes and flaked kippers. Season, if necessary, and spoon the mixture into the avocado shells.

6. In a small bowl combine the Parmesan cheese with the breadcrumbs. Mix well and sprinkle the filled avocados with the mixture. Cook under a preheated medium hot grill for 2-3 minutes until golden.

Microspot: *lemons will yield more juice if they are lightly pricked and warmed on HIGH in the microwave cooker for a few seconds.*

To freeze: *not suitable for freezing.*

Right Pork and apple en croûte (page 72); *Far right* Layered berry and ice cream cups (page 72); *Bottom* Avocados with smoked fish

PORK AND APPLE EN CROÛTE

SERVES 6
PREPARATION & COOKING TIME: 30 Minutes

1 tablespoon oil
6 frozen boneless pork loin steaks, thawed
1 tablespoon butter
100 g (4 oz) frozen onion slices, or 1 small fresh onion, peeled and sliced
250 g (8 oz) frozen Bramley apple slices
pinch of dried sage
salt
freshly ground black pepper
2 × 225 g (8 oz) frozen puff pastry, thawed
1 egg, beaten

1. Heat the oil in a frying pan, add the loin steaks and quickly seal them on both sides.

2. With a fish slice, transfer the loin steaks to a plate and set aside to cool. Add the butter and the onions to the fat remaining in the frying pan and cook over medium heat until the onions are soft. Add the apple slices and sage and stir-fry over gentle heat for 2-3 minutes. Season to taste.

3. On a floured board, roll out each piece of pastry to a rectangle measuring approximately 15×46 cm (6×18 inches) and cut each into 3 squares.

4. Place a pork steak left of centre on each square of pastry. Spoon the onion and apple mixture on top. Brush the pastry edges with water and fold over the pastry to make neat parcels. Seal the edges well and trim if necessary. Brush the top of each pastry parcel with beaten egg. Re-roll the pastry trimmings and use to decorate the parcels.

5. Carefully transfer the pastry parcels to a baking sheet and bake in a preheated hot oven (220°C, 425°F, Gas Mark 7) for 15-20 minutes until puffed and golden.

6. Serve with mange tout peas and baby potatoes, if liked.

Microspot: *to thaw the pork in the microwave cooker, follow the instructions under Pork loin steaks with mustard cream sauce (page 56). To thaw the pastry, follow the instructions under Camembert parcels with sour cherry sauce (page 16).*

To freeze: *open freeze the uncooked parcels, then wrap in foil and freeze for up to 1 month. To serve, unwrap and place on a damp baking sheet. Cook from frozen in a preheated hot oven (230°C, 450°F, Gas Mark 8) for 20 minutes; then reduce the temperature to moderately hot (200°C, 400°F, Gas Mark 6) for 20 minutes more or until golden brown.*

LAYERED BERRY AND ICE CREAM CUPS

SERVES 6
PREPARATION TIME: 10 Minutes

1.5 litres (2½ pints) vanilla ice cream
450 g (1 lb) frozen raspberries, thawed
225 g (8 oz) frozen strawberries, partially thawed
150 ml (¼ pint) frozen whipping cream, partially thawed
50 g (2 oz) almond flakes, toasted

1. Layer scoops of vanilla ice cream into 6 individual sundae dishes.

2. Mix the berries together in a medium bowl. Divide between the sundae dishes and top each with a further scoop of ice cream.

3. Lightly whip the cream and add a little to each dish.

4. Sprinkle with toasted almond flakes and serve.

Microspot: *to toast the almond flakes in the microwave cooker, follow the instructions under Raspberry almond bombe (page 40). For instructions on partially thawing strawberries, see Marbled strawberry cream (page 41) and to thaw the raspberries, refer to Raspberry croûtes (page 41), increasing the time to 5-6 minutes.*

To freeze: *not suitable for freezing.*

CHICKEN SCHNITZELS WITH LEMON AND GARLIC

SERVES 6
PREPARATION & COOKING TIME: 22 Minutes

6 frozen chicken breast portions, thawed, skinned and boned
175 g (6 oz) butter
1 tablespoon oil
1 clove garlic, crushed
1 tablespoon wholegrain mustard
6 tablespoons lemon juice
4 tablespoons chopped fresh parsley

1. Place each of the chicken breasts between 2 sheets of greaseproof paper. Beat with a rolling pin to flatten them slightly.

2. Melt 1 tablespoon of the butter in the oil in a heavy-based frying pan until the butter begins to turn to a light golden brown.

3. Immediately add the chicken breasts in a single layer and fry over high heat for 2-3 minutes on each side, until they are golden brown and cooked right through.

4. Transfer the chicken to a serving dish, cover and keep hot.

5. Wipe out the frying pan with paper towels, then add the rest of the butter, the garlic and the mustard. Stir-fry over a gentle heat for 2 minutes and then stir in the lemon juice and parsley.

6. Heat gently, spoon over the chicken and serve immediately.

Variation: *heat the butter and garlic for the sauce and stir in 1 teaspoon of plain flour. Cook for 1 minute, then add the remaining ingredients with 150 ml (¼ pint) soured cream.*

Microspot: *to thaw the chicken in the microwave cooker, follow the instructions under Breasts of chicken with baby onions (page 26).*

To freeze: *follow instructions under Breast of chicken with baby onions (page 26).*

MENU 2

Smoked mackerel fillets
with horseradish sauce

Chicken schnitzels with lemon
and garlic

Double chocolate and cherry
sundae

SMOKED MACKEREL FILLETS WITH HORSERADISH SAUCE

SERVES 6
PREPARATION & COOKING TIME: 15 Minutes

6 frozen mackerel fillets, thawed
6 sprigs fresh dill or fennel
1 tablespoon lemon juice
1 tablespoon olive oil
salt
freshly ground black pepper
225 g (8 oz) low fat soft cheese
1 tablespoon creamed horseradish
1 tablespoon chopped fresh chives
brown bread and butter to serve

1. Arrange the mackerel fillets on 6 individual serving plates, adding a sprig of dill or fennel to each.

2. In a small bowl, combine the lemon juice, oil and seasoning. Mix well and spoon over the fish.

3. In a second bowl, mix the cheese, horseradish and chopped chives together. Serve the fish with triangles of thinly sliced brown bread and butter and hand the sauce separately.

Microspot: *to thaw the mackerel fillets, arrange them on a plate, thin ends to centre, cover and microwave on DEFROST for 7-8 minutes per 450 g (1 lb). Allow to STAND for 5 minutes.*

To freeze: *not suitable for freezing.*

DOUBLE CHOCOLATE AND CHERRY SUNDAE

SERVES 6
PREPARATION TIME: 10 Minutes
1.5 litres (2½ pints) American rich chocolate ice cream
500 ml (18 fl oz) vanilla ice cream
450 g (1 lb) frozen dark cherries, thawed
150 ml (¼ pint) whipping cream, lightly whipped
100 g (4 oz) crumbled chocolate flake bars

1. Spoon scoops of chocolate and vanilla ice cream into 6 individual sundae glasses.

2. Add the cherries.

3. Spoon over cream and sprinkle with the chocolate flake.

Microspot: *to thaw the cherries in the microwave cooker, follow the instructions under Chocolate ice cream torte (page 40), increasing the thawing time to 7-9 minutes.*

To freeze: *not suitable for freezing.*

Above left Chicken schnitzels with lemon and garlic (page 73); *Right* Double chocolate and cherry sundae

---

MENU 3
Fried onion rings with spring onion dip
Spicy haddock korma
Lychee and orange cup

FRIED ONION RINGS WITH SPRING ONION DIP

SERVES 6
PREPARATION & COOKING TIME: 25 Minutes
225 g (8 oz) low fat soft cheese
1 tablespoon mayonnaise
1 tablespoon natural yogurt
6 spring onions, finely chopped
salt
freshly ground black pepper
2 tablespoons chopped fresh parsley
oil for deep frying
1 kg (2¼ lb) frozen crispy-coated onion rings

1. In a bowl, combine the cheese, mayonnaise, yogurt and spring onions. Stir together until thoroughly mixed and season to taste with salt and freshly ground black pepper.

. Spoon into a small shallow dish and prinkle with parsley.

. Just before serving, heat the oil in a large aucepan or deep-fat fryer to 180-190°C 350-375°F) or until a cube of bread browns in 30 seconds. Add one third of the onions in atter and fry until golden and crisp. Drain vell on paper towels while frying the rest of the onions in 2 batches. Drain them noroughly and serve in heaps on individual lates with the dip.

Microspot: *softened cheese is easier to mix. ollow the instructions under Cheese and weet pepper spread (page 51).*

o freeze: *not suitable for freezing.*

SPICY HADDOCK KORMA

SERVES 6
PREPARATION & COOKING TIME: 30 Minutes

4 tablespoons oil
1 teaspoon finely chopped fresh root ginger
2 green chilis, sliced lengthways and chopped, or ½ teaspoon chili powder
150 g (5 oz) frozen onion slices, or 1 medium fresh onion, peeled and sliced
1 clove garlic, crushed
½ teaspoon ground turmeric
½ teaspoon coriander seeds, crushed
5 ripe tomatoes, skinned and chopped
8 × 75 g (3 oz) frozen haddock steaks, thawed and cubed
225 g (8 oz) frozen Ocean Stix, thawed and flaked
salt
150 ml (¼ pint) soured cream
fresh coriander leaves, chopped, to garnish

1. Heat the oil in a large saucepan and stir in the ginger and chilis. Allow the mixture to brown slightly for 10 seconds.

2. Add the onion and garlic and fry for 2 minutes, until the onion is soft.

3. Add the turmeric and crushed coriander seeds and stir-fry for 1 minute.

4. Stir in the tomatoes, reduce the heat, cover and simmer for 15 minutes.

5. Add the haddock and Ocean Stix with salt to taste. Cover and simmer very gently for 5 minutes until the haddock flakes easily when tested with a fork.

6. Stir in the soured cream and heat gently. Pour into a serving dish, sprinkle with coriander leaves and serve with rice.

Microspot: *to thaw the fish steaks, follow the instructions under Curried fish scramble (page 54).*

To freeze: *not suitable for freezing.*

Left Spicy haddock korma

LYCHEE AND ORANGE CUP

SERVES 6
PREPARATION & COOKING TIME: 20 Minutes

567 g (20 oz) can lychees, drained, juice reserved
1 tablespoon gelatine
200 ml (7 fl oz) frozen concentrated Jaffa orange juice, measured after dilution
1 tablespoon lemon juice
1 tablespoon honey
150 ml (¼ pint) thick set natural yogurt
fresh rose petals to decorate (optional)

1. Cut the lychees in half and set aside. Place 4 tablespoons of the reserved lychee juice in a cup and sprinkle the gelatine on top. Leave until the gelatine becomes spongy.

2. Heat the remaining lychee juice in a medium saucepan over gentle heat, add the gelatine mixture and stir until it has dissolved.

3. Add the orange and lemon juice and the honey. Stir well and chill until the jelly begins to set.

4. Fold in the yogurt and lychees.

5. Spoon into a shallow serving dish and sprinkle with rose petals to serve.

Microspot: *to dissolve the gelatine in the microwave cooker, place the lychee juice in a cup as in Step 1, sprinkle the gelatine on top and microwave on MEDIUM for 30-45 seconds. Stir until the gelatine has dissolved.*

To freeze: *not suitable for freezing.*

MENU 4

Crumbed cauliflower pots

Nasi goreng

Apple flambé

CRUMBED CAULIFLOWER POT'

SERVES 4
PREPARATION & COOKING TIME: 22 Minutes

450 g (1 lb) frozen cauliflower
50 g (2 oz) butter
2 tablespoons plain flour
300 ml (½ pint) creamy milk
salt
freshly ground black pepper
175 g (6 oz) Cheddar cheese, grated
6 tablespoons fresh white breadcrumbs

1. Bring a saucepan of water to the boil, ad the cauliflower and cook for 6-8 minutes until just tender. Drain well and divide th florets between 4 small heatproof dishes ramekins.

2. Melt half the butter in a small saucepar Stir in the flour and cook for 1 minute withou browning. Gradually add the milk and brin to the boil, stirring constantly until the sauc is smooth and thick. Season well and stir i the cheese.

3. Divide the sauce between the dishes coating the cauliflower.

4. Melt the remaining butter in a sma saucepan, add the breadcrumbs and mi well. Sprinkle the crumb mixture over th cauliflower and place the dishes under preheated grill for 3-4 minutes until th topping is golden and bubbling. Serv immediately.

Microspot: *for a perfect cheese sauce warm the milk in a jug in the microwav cooker for 1½-2 minutes on HIGH befor stirring it into the flour and butter.*

o freeze: *freeze without the crumb topping.
:ool quickly, wrap the dishes in foil and
eeze for up to 3 months. To serve, thaw for
-2 hours. Reheat in a preheated moderately
ot oven (190°C, 375°F, Gas Mark 5) for
0-15 minutes, then make the topping,
prinkle it over the dishes and proceed as
irected above.*

ʌASI GORENG

ERVES 4
REPARATION & COOKING TIME: 30 Minutes
-6 tablespoons oil
25 g (8 oz) frozen onion slices, or 2 small fresh
nions, peeled and sliced
clove garlic, crushed
teaspoon ground coriander
teaspoon fresh root ginger, chopped
inch of chili powder
00 g (4 oz) frozen shelled prawns
50 g (5 oz) cooked ham, chicken or pork, cut into
in strips
00 g (4 oz) frozen peas
25 g (8 oz) frozen long grain rice, thawed
oy sauce
alt
O GARNISH:
one-egg omelettes, cooked like pancakes, then
olled up and cut into strips
-3 spring onions, cut into strips
fresh chili peppers, seeded and cut into
iamonds (optional)

. Heat 4 tablespoons oil in a large frying
an or wok and fry the onion for 3-5 minutes
ntil soft and just beginning to colour. Add
ne garlic, coriander, ginger and chili powder
nd stir-fry for 1-2 minutes more, adding a
ttle more oil if necessary.

. Add the prawns and stir-fry for 30
econds.

. Stir in the meat, peas and rice, with a little
nore oil if needed. Cook over medium heat,
tirring constantly, for 3-4 minutes until the
nixture is piping hot.

. Season to taste with soy sauce and salt
nd spread on to a large serving dish or oval
latter.

5. Garnish with rolls of omelette, onions and
chili peppers. Serve with extra soy or chili
sauce and fried bananas, if liked.

To freeze: *not suitable for freezing.*

Microspot: *to thaw the rice in the microwave
cooker, tip it into a bowl, cover loosely and
microwave for 3-4 minutes on DEFROST,
separating the grains once with a fork. Allow
to STAND until completely thawed.*

APPLE FLAMBÉ

SERVES 4
PREPARATION & COOKING TIME: 25 Minutes
450 g (1 lb) frozen Bramley apple slices, partially
thawed
2 tablespoons honey
1 tablespoon butter
3-4 tablespoons caster sugar
2 tablespoons brandy, warmed

1. Arrange the apple slices in a shallow
heatproof dish, packing them in tightly.

2. Dribble the honey over the apples and dot
with small flakes of butter.

3. Place the dish about 10 cm (4 inches)
below a preheated grill and cook for about
10 minutes or until the juices bubble and the
apples are just soft.

4. Remove from the grill and sprinkle the top
thickly with sugar. Return to the grill for 3-5
minutes until the sugar caramelizes to a rich
golden brown.

5. At the table, pour over the warmed
brandy and flame carefully. Serve with
cream, ice cream or custard.

Microspot: *to warm the brandy in the
microwave cooker follow the instructions
under Stilton steakgrills (page 28).*

To freeze: *not suitable for freezing.*

TOMATO AND BASIL SOUP

SERVES 6
PREPARATION & COOKING TIME: 16 Minutes

25 g (1 oz) butter
1 tablespoon oil
150 g (5 oz) frozen onion slices, or 1 medium fresh onion, peeled and sliced
3 tablespoons plain flour
794 g (28 oz) can chopped tomatoes
350 ml (12 fl oz) boiling water
1 chicken stock cube
1 tablespoon tomato purée
salt
freshly ground black pepper
2 teaspoons chopped fresh basil leaves
150 ml (¼ pint) single cream

1. Melt the butter in the oil in a large saucepan and fry the onion for 2-3 minutes.

2. Stir in the flour and cook for 1 minute. Add the tomatoes with their juice and mix well. In a jug, mix the boiling water with the stock cube. Stir the stock into the pan with the tomato purée and season to taste. Bring to the boil, reduce the heat and simmer for 5 minutes.

3. Purée in a blender or food processor or press through a sieve. Return the soup to the pan, check the seasoning and stir in the basil and cream. Heat gently and serve.

Microspot: *fresh basil can be dried in the microwave cooker. Follow the instructions under Fish steaks en papillote (page 30).*

To freeze: *follow the instructions under Cream of asparagus soup (page 10).*

POACHED WHOLE SALMON WITH LEMON MAYONNAISE

SERVES 6
PREPARATION & COOKING TIME: 30 Minutes

2 litres (3½ pints) water or a mixture of water and dry white wine, e.g. Muscadet
100 g (4 oz) frozen onion slices or 1 small fresh onion, peeled and sliced
1 bay leaf
1 small stick celery, chopped
small bunch of parsley
12 peppercorns
2 tablespoons vinegar or lemon juice
salt
1.25-1.5 kg (2½-3 lb) frozen whole salmon, thawed
sprigs of watercress or parsley to garnish
FOR THE MAYONNAISE:
2 egg yolks, at room temperature
½ teaspoon made mustard
salt
freshly ground white pepper
200 ml (7 fl oz) olive or salad oil
1 tablespoon lemon juice
2 teaspoons boiling water

1. Put the water or wine, the onion, bay leaf celery, parsley, peppercorns, vinegar o lemon juice and salt into a fish kettle or large saucepan and bring to the boil.

2. Reduce the heat to a gentle simmer and carefully lower the salmon into the liquid Simmer for 5-7 minutes per 450 g (1 lb).

3. Place the egg yolks in a clean bowl and add the mustard and seasoning. Graduall beat in the oil, a drop at a time, and stir in the lemon juice and water.

5. Drain the fish and transfer it to a serving plate. Carefully remove the skin and garnish with watercress or parsley.

Microspot: *to thaw the whole salmon in the microwave cooker, prick the skin and microwave on DEFROST for 15-18 minutes shielding the head and tail with small pieces of foil if permitted in your microwave cooker. Allow to STAND for 5 minutes.*

To freeze: *not suitable for freezing.*

PINEAPPLE CARAMELS

SERVES 6
PREPARATION TIME: 15 Minutes

1.5 litres (2½ pints) vanilla ice cream
339 g (12 oz) can pineapple cubes
2 tablespoons Kirsch
150 g (5 oz) caster sugar
5 tablespoons water

1. Scoop the ice cream into 6 individual stainless steel dessert dishes.

2. Return the dishes to the freezer until just before serving.

3. When ready to serve, spoon the drained pineapple over the ice cream.

4. Heat the sugar, water and Kirsch in a small saucepan until the sugar has dissolved. Bring the mixture to the boil. Cook until the syrup turns a pale golden colour. Do not stir, but gently shake the saucepan as the syrup starts to darken. Quickly remove the syrup from the heat and carefully pour the caramel over the ice cream and pineapple. It will harden on contact. Serve immediately.

Microspot: *caramel can be made in the microwave cooker. Combine the sugar and water in a large heatproof glass jug and microwave on HIGH for 8-10 minutes until a caramel forms. Use oven gloves to remove the jug from the cooker – it will be hot. Carefully stir in 2 tablespoons of warm water (the mixture may spatter) and microwave on HIGH for 30 seconds more.*

To freeze: *not suitable for freezing.*

Below Poached whole salmon with lemon mayonnaise

INDEX